Diary of a Se
Swinton Lions
2021

Stuart Latham

Diary of a Season – Swinton Lions 2021

Stuart Latham

ISBN number: 978-1-8381165-8-3

Printed and bound by CPI Group (UK) Ltd, Croydon, CR0 4YY
Published by: S & T Sales and Marketing Ltd, Sale, Cheshire M33 4QN

Other Books from the same author:
Ice Hockey in Solihull – ISBN No - 978-1-8384609-5-2
A Kick in the Grass – ISBN No: 9780953060801
A Love That Refused to Die – ISBN No: - 0-9530608-1-0
The History of Chalfont St Peter AFC – ISBN No:9780953060825
Roughriders – The City of London Yeomanry During the First World War.
– ISBN No:9780953060849
The History of Ice Hockey in Peterborough ISBN No: 978-0-9530608-6-3
The History of the Swindon Wildcats 1986 – 2016 ISBN No: 978-0-9530608-7-0
The History of the Swindon Wildcats 1986 – 2012 ISBN No; 9780953060832
The History of the Bracknell Bees ISBN No 978-0-9530608-8-7
The City of London Yeomanry 1907-1918 ISBN: 978-0-9530608-5-6
March F1 – The Leyton House Years - 1987 – 1993 ISBN No: 978-0-9530608-9-4
Hadrian Bayley The Man Who Accepted the Surrender of Jerusalem
ISBN: 978-1-8381165-1-4
60 Years of The Altrincham Aces ISBN No: 978-1-8381165-0-7
The Deeside Dragons ISBN No: 978-1-8381165-3-8
Ice Hockey in Bristol ISBN No: 978-1-8381165-2-1
The Manchester Storm ISBN No: 978-1-8381165-4-5
Chalfont St Peter AFC 1926-2020 ISBN No: 978-1-8381165-5-2
The Rise and Fall of the Manchester Phoenix ISBN No: 978-1-8381165-6-9
Always and Forever ISBN No: 978-1-8381165-7-6
The Cardiff Devils – ISBN No: 978-1-8381165-9-0
Ice Hockey Memories – ISBN No: 978-1-8383328-0-8
The Slough Jets – ISBN No 978-1-8383328-2-2
The City of London Yeomanry Through Old Photographs – ISBN No: 978-1-8383328-3-9
More Ice Hockey Memories – ISBN No: 978-1-8383328-4-6
Ice Hockey in Edinburgh – ISBN No: 978-1-8383328-5-3
Wilmslow Cricket Club 75th Anniversary – ISBN No: 978-1-8383328-6-0
An Alternative View of the World of Cricket – ISBN No 978-1-8383328-7-7
Into the Abyss – ISBN No 978-1-8383328-8-4
Stars Wars– Oxford City Stars – ISBN No: 978-1-8383328-9-1
Swindon Ice Hockey Statistically Speaking 1986-2021 – ISBN No: 978-1-8384609-0-7
In Their Own Words - Swindon Ice Hockey Memories – ISBN No: 978-1-8384609-1-4
The Royal Tournament – A Pictorial History – ISBN No: 978-1-8384609-2-1
Hockey in Haringey – ISBN No: 978-1-8384609-3-8
From Vikings to Devils - Ice Hockey on the Solent – ISBN No: 978-1-8384609-4-5
Further details available from: Stuartlatham65@sky.com

Contents

Introduction

I was always a fan of the round ball until 1977 when my late father was promoted at work and we relocated to Alloa in Scotland. I then studied at Alloa Academy, which was a good school, but they did not have a football team, preferring athletics in the summer and rugby union in the winter. So, I took up rugby and athletics and between both became fairly good at it representing my school, county and even Central Region schools in Scotland, even having a trial for Scotland schoolboys, although unsuccessful I enjoyed playing and much to the annoyance of my classmates supporting England when the Nation visited Murrayfield, especially in 1980 when Bill Beaumont led England to the triple crown.

At this time, we had no mobile phones, no satellite TV and had to suffer only a couple of channels on the TV. So, when that came to sport, I had Sportscene and Scotsport, which mainly showed curling and football but being in Scotland that meant mostly Rangers and Celtic, and if you were lucky a few other teams from the Scottish Premier League. There was no Match of the Day as the focus was on Scotland and wrestling was shown on a Saturday afternoon. But one spark of interest was a weekly programme on BBC2 when the BBC showed the Floodlight Trophy that they sponsored, so watching on an old black and white tv in my bedroom I was introduced to the world of rugby league. I came to enjoy watching the programme and look

forward to watching mostly Hull and Hull Kingston Rovers (the BBC seemed to like covering these two teams!). I became hooked as I could see that league was more interesting than union and I  started to watch every programme.

I moved back to England in 1982 and living down south and with the BBC having stopped their trophy coverage I struggled to find any coverage of rugby league so returned to football which became my second occupation as I rose to play at a high level and also take jobs off the pitch as well. It was whilst I was attached to Reading FC that rugby re-emerged into my life as Richmond RFC played their last season in the union's premiership before collapsing and then being replaced by London Irish and as they shared the same ground as Reading FC, I used to pop along and get involved behind the scenes. But still no rugby league, so when my life was turned upside down 10 years ago through no fault of my own, I found myself having to find somewhere to live so chose Broughton, just over the Welsh border as I had a work contract with Airbus at the time. Queensferry was a few minutes' drive away and at Deeside Leisure Centre I found the Falcons rugby league side as well as the office of the Welsh rugby league so I had everything, I could watch ice hockey, Rugby league and football all within minutes of where I was living. So, when the 2013 Rugby League World Cup came to England and Wales I was in my element and whilst watching Wales lose to the USA at the Racecourse ground in Wrexham with a few friends realised that the Crusaders were close by and I could watch something decent all year round.

However, just as I was enjoying life again, I remarried, and my wife didn't like the local schools and wanted a decent school for her son to attend so we all moved to the Altrincham area for the schools and settled in Sale. She got what she wanted, and her son now attends Altrincham Grammar School for Boys and I managed to blend into the community and watch Ice Hockey in

Altrincham, the local football sides and by luck find out that the Swinton Lions had relocated also to Heywood Road, so I could have my live sport.

Work got in the way and I spent more time than I wanted working all over the country as well as abroad, but I had found what I had been missing in my life, a community and a sense of belonging in the Lions. I could  only attend at best 6 matches a season due to my other commitments but each time I ventured down to Heywood Road, I would always see the same friendly faces ready to chat and make the visit a pleasurable experience and I took the opportunity to promote the team by wearing the colours whenever I was abroad working. It certainly brought a few comments from people, especially in China!

I sponsored a Swinton player, whom I won't mention as his attitude was a disgrace and when he left the club, his replacement was no better and it soured things for me and I was at the point of giving up and going to watch Salford play when I came into contact with Andy Mazey and Steve Wild. Through them I could see that the club had a vision and with the fantastic loyal fans, a basis for development so I stayed and that is a decision I will never regret making as I found the perfect player to sponsor in Will Hope. The exact opposite of my previous experiences as he was committed to the club, had a family background associated with Swinton and was and still is a fantastic ambassador for the club. He even took time out to come to introduce himself to my wife at last season's season launch, completely unprompted and that speaks volumes for the person and when other players also take time out to openly chat and show interest in people because they want to talk rather than they have been told to mingle and chat shows how far the club has come on and off the pitch!

Andy may have left the club, but in his replacement, Stuart Fletcher, the club has gained someone with even more passion for the Lions and if you discount his supporting Stockport County, you will find someone with good judgement and who alongside Steve Wild will ensure the club survives and goes from strength to strength.

Whilst working away I wrote books and have had 20 published so far. In October 2020 I was sat in a bar in Exeter having a drink with Stuart Fletcher discussing promoting sports teams to the public and I told him of my experiences of how other clubs' attitudes were poor and how they had failed giving a few examples from personal experience when this book idea came to me. Steve Wild has covered the club's history in depth, so this book is for the fans covering the 2021 season and approaching the club from a new angle.

A percentage of the book revenue will go back into the club, so by buying this book, you are contributing to the running of the team, so thank you for your support. I hope you enjoy reading what went on during this season.

Stuart Latham
November 2021

Acknowledgements

We would like to acknowledge the following people:
End of Season Stats with thanks to Alan Dixon

Steve Wild	Allan Coleman	Rhys Griffiths
Stuart Fletcher	Ian Bailey	Stephen Parker
Cover Design by:	Katie Wild	Tracey Parker
Photography by	Pete Green	and	Emily J. Parker
Match Reports by:	Ian Rigg	Rhodri Lloyd

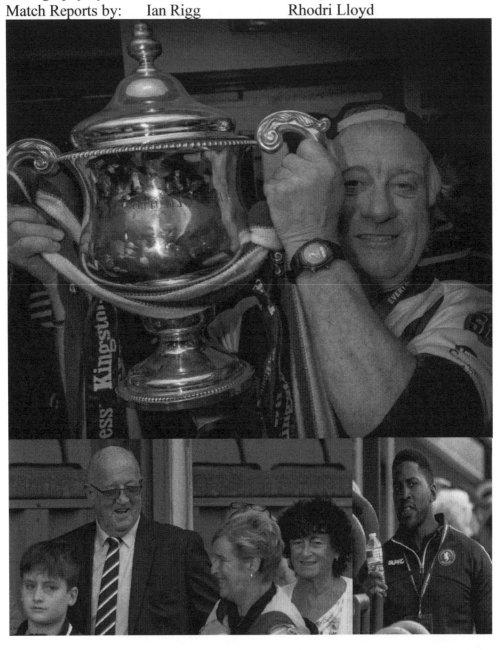

Subscribers List

We would like to thank the following for subscribing to this book:

Mark Cull	David Thomson	Alf Seddon
Nadya Familnova	Rhodri Lloyd	Stuart Fletcher
Steve Wild	Pete Green	Tracy Parker
Katie Wild	Victoria Salomon	Will Hope
Ian Bailey	Rhys Griffiths	Emily Parker
John Pitchford	Stephen Johnson	Mark Richardson
Stephen Parker	Sue Buckley-Howell	

The following player stats are from the start of the season.

The Players
RHODRI LLOYD

SECOND-ROW OR CENTRE
D.O.B 22, July 1993
JOINED CLUB 01/03/2015
Club skipper and Welsh international
Rhodri played a pivotal role for Swinton
in 2018, a season which he finished with
two crucial tries against Workington
Town in the play-off final. His
performances earned him multiple awards
at the Lions' end of season presentation
night – including the Fans' Player of the
Year, the Coaches' Player of the Year
and the Players' Player of the Year.

As the youngest player ever to be capped for Wales, he has also become a
key performer for his country. He played a starring role for the Dragons in
the 2018 European Championship, as well as appearing in the 2017 World
Cup. He originally made his Swinton debut on DR from Wigan during our
promotion campaign of 2015, before returning on a permanent basis in 2016.
In 2019, Rhodri scored six tries in 24 appearances for the Lions.
Season 2021 will be Rhodri's sixth full season with the Lions, where his all-
action style and never-say-die spirit have made him one of the most popular
players with the fans.
SQUAD NUMBER : 11
Swinton Stats: Heritage Number 1194; **Appearances** 118; **Tries** 36.
PREVIOUS CLUBS Wigan Warriors, London Broncos (loan), Workington
Town (loan), Whitehaven (loan).

My hopes are to progress on finishing 9th in 2019. Looking forward to
developing the club even further and hoping that we can achieve a top half
finish.

Autograph

LUKE WATERWORTH

HOOKER
D.O.B 20, June 1996
JOINED CLUB 26/06/2016

Luke first came to the Lions in mid-2016 on loan from Wigan Warriors, before committing on a permanent contract from the start of the 2017 season. It was during the 2017 campaign that he won the club's Try of the Season award, with the late effort which famously knocked Super League Huddersfield out of the Challenge Cup. Luke's consistent and solid displays have made him a firm favourite with Swinton supporters, and he rounded off the 2018 season with two crucial tries against Workington Town in the play-off final. In 2019 his displays at hooker continued to be consistently impressive, and he ended the campaign with three tries in 27 appearances. Season 2021 will be Luke's sixth with the Lions, during which no doubt he will pass the 100 appearances barrier.

SQUAD NUMBER : 9

Swinton Stats: Heritage Number 1224; **Appearances** 94; **Tries** 14.

PREVIOUS CLUBS Wigan Warriors

Autograph

JACK HANSEN

FULL BACK
D.O.B 12, January 1997
JOINED CLUB 20/08/2017

Jack's performances at both full-back and half-back earned him the Lions' 2018 Young Player of the Year award. The son of former Swinton favourite Lee Hansen, Jack first broke through the ranks at the Leigh East community club. He then joined the Leigh Centurions set up as an 18-year-old, from where he gained experience with North Wales Crusaders whilst on loan. He joined Swinton at a difficult time in late 2017, before asserting himself in the Swinton starting line-up from the start of the 2018 campaign. During the 2019 season Jack developed as one of the most consistent half-backs in the Championship, and his 29 appearances were the most by any Swinton player. At the End of Season Presentation Evening, Jack won a special award for his touchline conversion which famously won the league fixture over in France, 20-18 against Toulouse Olympique. Jack recently penned a two-year deal with the Lions, and will be looking to establish devastating half-back partnership with Martyn Ridyard

SQUAD NUMBER : 6
Swinton Stats: Heritage Number 1250; **Appearances** 57; **Tries** 11; **Goals** 64.

PREVIOUS CLUBS Leigh East ARLFC, Leigh Centurions, North Wales Crusaders (loan)

Autograph

BRANDON WOOD

WING
D.O.B 31, July 2000
JOINED CLUB 01/12/2019

Outside-back Brandon joined the Lions to balance the squad following the departure of Matty Ashton to Warrington late in the 2019 season. Like Ashton, Brandon is a product of community club Rochdale Mayfield, whilst he also spent time in the Bradford Bulls academy set up.

He signed his first professional contract with Rochdale Hornets after impressing during a trial period and went on to score an impressive ten tries in his debut year in the Championship for the Hornets. With youth on his side, Brandon is an outstanding prospect.

Brandon left the club to concentrate on his business commitments outside of rugby in December 2020.

SQUAD NUMBER : 5

Swinton Stats : Heritage Number 0; **Appearances** 0; **Tries** 0.

PREVIOUS CLUBS Bradford Bulls (academy), Rochdale Mayfield ARLFC, Rochdale Hornets

Autograph

MITCH COX

CENTRE
D.O.B 15, November 1993
JOINED CLUB 01/12/2019

Mitch, a centre, joined Swinton from Leigh Centurions ahead of the 2020 campaign. He made 11 appearances and scored six tries during the 2019 season for the Leythers. Mitch has also featured in the National Conference League for both Leigh Miners Rangers and Thatto Heath, in addition to which he has also spent a season in Australia playing for the Thirroul Butchers club based in Wollongong. Mitch is highly regarded by both Head Coach Stuart Littler and his assistant Allan Coleman, both of whom have coached him previously. He played in all 5 of the Lions' competitive games in early 2020, scoring 3 tries in the process.

SQUAD NUMBER : 3

Swinton Stats : Heritage Number 1289; **Appearances** 5; **Tries** 3.

PREVIOUS CLUBS Thirroul Butchers (Australia), North Wales Crusaders, Leigh Centurions

Autograph

DEANE MEADOWS

FORWARD
D.O.B 11, May 1994
JOINED CLUB 02/08/2019

Deane joined the Lions during the summer of 2019 from community club Shevington Sharks following a successful trial period, but has had to wait patiently for his senior debut. Earlier in 2019 he toured Jamaica with the North West English Lionhearts, and was also a member of the Lancashire BARLA side which travelled to Serbia in May to play Red Star Belgrade. Deane previously emerged with the North West Men's Premier League side Shevington Sharks. He can cover a variety of positions and adds good value to the Lions' squad. Deane is yet to make his full Swinton debut, but he did score a try in the pre-season victory at Bradford Bulls in early 2021

SQUAD NUMBER : 19

Swinton Stats : Heritage Number 0; **Appearances** 0; **Tries** 0.

PREVIOUS CLUBS Shevington Sharks ARLFC

Autograph

BEN HEYES

FULL-BACK
D.O.B 5, October 1998
JOINED CLUB 01/12/2019

Young full-back Ben joined the
Lions in November 2019 from the
premier amateur club, Thatto Heath.
He was prominent in that club's
impressive 2019 Challenge Cup run,
during which they defeated League 1
side North Wales Crusaders before
suffering a close defeat to Dewsbury
Rams in the fifth round. Ben also
took part in the 2019 England
Community Lions' ground-breaking
tour to New Zealand, and won the
man-of-the-match award in the

Second Test. Ben is a young, exciting player who has bags of pace and
potential, and another who fits the club's recruitment profile perfectly. He
made his Lions' debut in the victory over Leigh Miners Rangers early in
2020.

SQUAD NUMBER : 21

Swinton Stats : Heritage Number 1294; **Appearances** 1; **Tries** 0.

PREVIOUS CLUBS Salford Reds (academy), Thatto Heath ARLFC

Autograph

TAYLER BROWN

SECOND ROW
D.O.B 16, October 1999
JOINED CLUB 01/12/2019

Tayler emerged through the Newton Storm amateur club as a youngster, before joining the Warrington Wolves development programme from the age of 15. He progressed impressively through the Wolves' Academy teams, for whom he established himself as a highly consistent performer. The young second-rower fits well into the Lions' club ethos of being young and hungry to progress. Tayler has a good frame and is tipped for a bright future in the game. He made his Lions' debut in the victory over Leigh Miners Rangers early in 2020

SQUAD NUMBER : 20

Swinton Stats : Heritage Number 1293; **Appearances** 1; **Tries** 0.

PREVIOUS CLUBS Newton Storm ARLFC, Warrington Wolves (academy

Autograph

RICHARD LEPORI

WING
D.O.B 21, October 1991
JOINED CLUB 06/06/2019

Richard arrived at the Lions half-way through the 2019 campaign, making his debut against Toronto Wolfpack at Heywood Road in early June. He scored his first Swinton try in the memorable 34-34 draw at Bradford, and added two more when the Lions comfortably beat Halifax towards the end of the season. Richard first started playing Rugby League with Chorley Panthers as a youngster, and from there earned a place on a Salford Reds scholarship scheme. He then moved into the professional game, and has seen extensive action during spells with Oldham, Whitehaven and (in 2018) Rochdale Hornets. He was actually playing Rugby Union with Sedgley Tigers when the Lions offered him a way back into the Championship, and it was an opportunity that the tough winger accepted with both hands. Being of half Italian heritage, Richard has also been proud to represent Italy, and he played for the Azurri in the 2017 World Cup.

SQUAD NUMBER : 2
Swinton Stats : Heritage Number 1286; **Appearances** 14; **Tries** 5.

PREVIOUS CLUBS Atherton Roosters (Australia), Oldham, Whitehaven, Rochdale Hornets, Sedgley Tigers RUFC

Autograph

SAM GRANT

CENTRE/WING
D.O.B 24, March 1999
JOINED CLUB 01/12/2019

Sam joined the Lions from Wigan
Warriors prior to the start of the
2020 season, having been an
integral cog in their successful
Academy teams. Grant, who can
play at either centre or wing, was
part of the Wigan u19s team that
was crowned Super League
Academy Champions in 2018.
During the 2019 season Sam
played on loan at London Skolars
and scored three tries in four
appearances, before going on to make two further outings with Rochdale
Hornets towards the end of the season. He made his Swinton debut in early
2020 just before the first lockdown, when he scored a try against Leigh
Miners Rangers in the Challenge Cup.

SQUAD NUMBER : 19

Swinton Stats : Heritage Number 1292; **Appearances** 3; **Tries** 1.

PREVIOUS CLUBS Wigan Warriors (academy)

Autograph

LOUIS BROGAN

FORWARD
D.O.B 6, May 2000
JOINED CLUB 01/12/2019

Salford-born Louis joined the Lions
from Leigh Miners Rangers,
following in the footsteps of Frankie
Halton. A highly promising young
forward with an athletic frame, Louis
can cover forward positions both as a
middle and in the back-row. In 2019
Louis represented England in the
European Youth Championships and
earned an award as 'Best Forward' in
the tournament. Added to that
accolade he was also named the 2019
'Player of Year' for Lancashire
Under 19s, as well as carrying off the

Leigh Miners Rangers' 'Young Player of the Year' award. Louis made his
full Swinton debut in the victory at Whitehaven in early 2020, and went on
to appear in all 5 of the Lions' competitive fixtures ahead of lockdown.

SQUAD NUMBER : 15

Swinton Stats : Heritage Number 1291; **Appearances** 5; **Tries** 0.

PREVIOUS CLUBS Leigh Miners Rangers ARLFC

Autograph

JOSE KENGA

PROP-FORWARD
D.O.B 3, May 1995
JOINED CLUB 01/12/2018

Jose was born at Kinshasa in the Democratic Republic of Congo, but played his early rugby with Hunslet Warriors in the South Leeds area. He then came under the wing of a scholarship programme at Leeds Rhinos, before joining Sheffield Eagles at the age of 16 early in 2012. After three years with the Eagles, Jose continued his development with Dewsbury Rams in their reserve side. Jose's break into first grade rugby league came with Hunslet in 2016, with whom he spent two seasons before transferring to Keighley Cougars for the 2018 season. Jose made a big impact at Cougar Park, and had come under the scrutiny of a number of clubs in the Championship before joining the Lions at the start of the 2019 campaign. Jose made 16 appearances during his Swinton debut season, and 3 more in early 2020.

SQUAD NUMBER : 17

Swinton Stats : Heritage Number 1278; **Appearances** 19; **Tries** 0

PREVIOUS CLUBS Hunslet Warriors ARLFC, Sheffield Eagles, Dewsbury Rams, Gloucestershire All Golds (loan), Hunslet, Keighley Cougars.

Autograph

PADDY JONES

FORWARD
D.O.B 7, February 1997
JOINED CLUB 01/07/2018

Paddy had an outstanding season during 2019, after which he deservedly carried off the club's Man of Steel award at the End of Season Presentation Night. This was just reward for his 27 consistent appearances during which time he produced tough and uncompromising performances and never took a backward step. Paddy is a Liverpudlian who first emerged through the Wigan Academy system, before enjoying a period playing in the French Elite League with Villeneuve Leopards. He has also had spells with Rochdale Hornets and Dewsbury Rams. Paddy played in 4 of the Lions' 2020 fixtures just prior to lockdown.

SQUAD NUMBER : 16

Swinton Stats: Heritage Number 1271; **Appearances** 43; **Tries** 1.

PREVIOUS CLUBS Wigan (Academy), Villeneuve Leopards, Rochdale Hornets, Dewsbury Rams.

Autograph

BILLY BRICKHILL

FORWARD
D.O.B 30, April 1997
JOINED CLUB 01/12/2018

After winning the Rochdale Hornets Young Player of the Year award in 2018, Billy's capture ahead of the 2019 season represented a significant piece of pre-season business for the Lions. Having started his career at community club Cadishead Rhinos, Billy might also be considered as being yet another local in the Swinton team. Billy featured for Lancashire Under 18s at amateur level, before gaining experience in the pro game with Gloucestershire All Golds and North Wales Crusaders. At the All Golds he won the Player of the Year award in 2017, and at Crusaders he won their 2016 Young Player of the Year. In 2016 he also played a single game for Doncaster. One of Billy's great attributes is that he can cover a variety of positions across the forward line. He is highly rated by the Swinton coaching staff, and a promising future seems assured especially at his current levels of progress in terms of commitment and consistency. These attributes came to the fore in 2019 when he scored a couple of tries in an impressive 27 appearances. Billy added two more appearances at the start of the 2020 campaign.

SQUAD NUMBER : 14
Swinton Stats : Heritage Number 1277; **Appearances** 29; **Tries** 2.

PREVIOUS CLUBS Cadishead Rhinos ARLFC, Doncaster, Gloucestershire All Golds, North West Crusaders, Rochdale Hornets.

Autograph

WILL HOPE

LOOSE-FORWARD
D.O.B 2, June 1993
JOINED CLUB 25/03/2018

Although Will did play in all 5
competitive Swinton games in early 2020,
he will still be looking for a belated fresh
start after suffering a devastating injury in
the 2019 season opener at Sheffield
Eagles. Thankfully he has made a good
recovery, and will continue to be proud to
represent his home-town club, following
in the footsteps of his grandfather Jim
Hope who played for Swinton between 1957 and 1966. Will made his
Swinton debut in March 2018 following a stint with Sheffield Eagles. He had
originally come through the Folly Lane ARLFC system before joining the
Salford Academy set up. He subsequently played four times for the Salford
first-team, before going on loan to Oldham and Sheffield Eagles during the
2013 and 2014 seasons. After joining Oldham on a permanent transfer he
helped the Roughyeds to the 2015 League 1 title. He spent 2016 with
Oldham in the Championship, before transferring to Sheffield Eagles for
2017. Through family connections Will qualifies for Ireland, and he played
for the Wolfhounds during both the 2017 World Cup and the 2018 European
Championships. He is undoubtedly a leader in the Swinton squad, and a
player of true Championship calibre. Will leads by example, with good ball
skills, an ability to make hard yards, and is clinical in the tackle. He will be
looking to finish the 2021 season by playing a prominent part for Ireland in
the World Cup.
SQUAD NUMBER : 13
Swinton Stats: Heritage Number 1264; **Appearances** 24; **Tries** 5.
PREVIOUS CLUBS Folly Lane ARLFC, Salford Red Devils, Oldham,
Sheffield Eagles

Autograph

LEWIS HATTON

FORWARD
D.O.B 14, January 1997
JOINED CLUB 01/12/2018
Lewis represented a major capture for the Lions ahead of the 2019 season, having arrived at Heywood Road from Rochdale Hornets. He is a forward that can keep going relentlessly for the full 80 minutes, which in itself is a rare ability in the modern game. Lewis played his early rugby league in the St Helens area before joining the under 19s set up at Salford. From there he went to Warrington Wolves, and spent time on loan with the Hornets during their promotion campaign of 2017. He then joined Rochdale on a permanent transfer for 2018, and scored four tries in 25 appearances for the Spotland club. Lewis had some impressive games against Swinton in 2018 for Hornets, where he won their coveted Player of the Year award, which made him a prime target for Head Coach Stuart Littler. In his debut season for the Lions in 2019, Lewis was consistently impressive with his direct and aggressive style. He scored two tries in 27 appearances, including one in a crucial 20-18 victory over Batley. Lewis played in all 5 of the Lions' competitive games of early 2020, and scored a crucial try in the fine victory up at Whitehaven. As a front-line worker with the NHS he has played a proud role in the fight against Covid-19.
SQUAD NUMBER : 10
Swinton Stats : Heritage Number 1275; **Appearances** 32; **Tries** 4.

PREVIOUS CLUBS Pilkington Recs ARLFC, Clock Face Miners ARLFC, St Helens Academy, Salford Academy, Warrington Wolves, Rochdale Hornets.

Autograph

MIKE BUTT

WING
D.O.B 6, May 1995
JOINED CLUB 17/05/2015

Mike originally joined the Lions on trialist forms from Manchester Metropolitan University in 2015, but impressed enough to quickly earn his first professional contract. A former England student international, Mike is now a well established and feared Championship outside-back. After winning the club's Young Player of the Year award in 2017, he followed this up by landing the Lions' prestigious Man of Steel award in 2018. He was Swinton's leading try scorer in 2017, and second top scorer in 2018. Mike's performances in 2018 were consistently solid, and prompted a call-up to the Wales squad for the 2018 European Championship for whom he qualifies by heritage. In the 2019 season he scored an impressive 22 tries in 27 appearances to finish as third top try scorer in the Championship. During the covid-impacted 2020 season Mike amassed an impressive 9 tries in 5 appearances, including 4 in the cup-tie against Leigh Miners Rangers. Season 2021 will be his seventh campaign with the club.

SQUAD NUMBER : 1

Swinton Stats : Heritage Number 1202; **Appearances** 110; **Tries** 66.

PREVIOUS CLUBS None

Autograph

SAM BROOKS

FORWARD
D.O.B 29, September 1993
JOINED CLUB 01/12/2020

Sam is a Wigan-born prop-forward with a proven track record of success at the top end of the Championship with Halifax, Featherstone Rovers and Leigh. Sam also gained Super League experience with Widnes, and is a full Scottish international. 26 years old Sam emerged through the academy system at Wigan before joining Halifax in 2014. He then had a spell with Whitehaven, before joining the then Super League outfit Widnes Vikings. In 2017 and 2018 he was one of the Championship's stand-out performers whilst with Featherstone Rovers, a reputation that he took to Leigh last year where he made 24 appearances. Sam is a non-nonsense and tough character, and will be looking to provide the forward momentum in the Lions' engine room.

SQUAD NUMBER : 8

Swinton Stats : Heritage Number 1296; **Appearances** 0; **Tries** 0.

PREVIOUS CLUBS Halifax, Whitehaven, Widnes, Featherstone Rovers, Leigh Centurions

Autograph

MARTYN RIDYARD

HALF-BACK
D.O.B 25, July 1986
JOINED CLUB 01/12/2020

Martyn is without doubt is one of the Rugby League Championship's most outstanding players of the past decade, and we were delighted to bring him to Heywood Road ahead of the 2021 season. An accomplished and experienced half-back, Martyn originally progressed through the community game at Leigh Miners Rangers, before earning his first professional contract in 2009 with his hometown club, Leigh Centurions. Martyn then enjoyed a stellar career at Leigh, during which time he earned a reputation as being one of the Championship's most exciting and influential performers. At Leigh he twice lifted the Northern Rail Cup, and then won the Man-of-the-Match award when Leigh carried off the Championship title in 2014. That same season Martyn was crowned the Kingstone Press Player of the Year. In 2017 Martyn spent an effective spell on loan at Super League Huddersfield, before joining Championship rivals Featherstone Rovers. He then returned to Leigh in 2019 and cemented his place as one of that club's all-time record points scorers.

SQUAD NUMBER : 6
Swinton Stats : Heritage Number 1295; **Appearances** 0; **Tries** 0.
PREVIOUS CLUBS Featherstone Rovers, Huddersfield Giants (loan), Leigh Centurions

Autograph

LIAM FORSYTH

CENTRE
D.O.B 23, March 1996
JOINED CLUB 01/12/2020

Liam joined Swinton on a two-year deal in late 2020 from Leigh Centurions, having already played 24 times for the Lions whilst on dual registration from Wigan between 2017 and 2019. During his Swinton DR period he scored 12 tries, with the highlights arguably being his two tries at Barrow in 2019 when the Lions won 33-26 to begin their ascent up the league table, and the scoring of a crucial try at Odsal against Bradford in August 2017 where the Lions won for the first time in 60 years. Liam has also had a spell at Bath RUFC, before joining Wigan in 2017 where he made 14 appearances at Super League level during which he scored 3 tries. He then joined Leigh at the start of the 2020 season and grabbed 10 tries in 10 outings ahead of lockdown and his switch to Heywood Road. Liam is an exceptional strike centre and a terrific addition to the squad.

SQUAD NUMBER : 4

Swinton Stats : Heritage Number 1229; **Appearances** 24; **Tries** 12.

PREVIOUS CLUBS Bath RUFC, Wigan Warriors, Leigh Centurions

Autograph

JORDAN BROWN

FORWARD
D.O.B 30, September 2000
JOINED CLUB 01/12/2020

Forward Jordan arrived at the Lions from Widnes Vikings late in 2020. He was born at Warrington and came through the junior ranks at the Wolves before signing for our Championship rivals Widnes. He is a good size athlete and can competently cover both the middle and back-row positions, and therefore provides genuine competition for places in the Lions' forward ranks.

SQUAD NUMBER : 26

Swinton Stats : Heritage Number 0; **Appearances** 0; **Tries** 0.

PREVIOUS CLUBS Warrington Wolves (academy); Widnes Vikings

Autograph

LUIS ROBERTS

SECOND-ROW
D.O.B 24, March 2002
JOINED CLUB 01/12/2020

Luis played for the Lions' Swinton-based community partner club Folly Lane ARLFC ahead of joining Salford Red Devils last year. Luis then appeared in the Reds' reserve grade team at the start of the 2020 season, and also saw brief first team action against the Lions during the pre-season friendly at the AJ Bell Stadium. Luis is a strong running second-row forward with a great attitude towards his own development. He was very highly thought of at Salford, and his recruitment could prove to be a very shrewd piece of business.

SQUAD NUMBER : 25

Swinton Stats : Heritage Number 0; **Appearances** 0; **Tries** 0.

PREVIOUS CLUBS Folly Lane ARLFC, Salford Red Devils

Autograph

PAUL NASH

HOOKER
D.O.B 16, April 2000
JOINED CLUB 01/12/2020

Paul began his junior career at Clock
Face, but soon moved to Blackbrook
from where he progressed to the
Saints' scholarship programme at the
age of 15. He then represented
England Youth against both Wales
and France, before moving up to the
St Helens Academy at the age of 17.
Paul was a member of the Saints
team that contested the Academy
Grand Final in 2019, whilst also
establishing himself as a key
performer in the St Helens reserve
team. Paul is a hooker with
outstanding promise, and fits perfectly into our recruitment profile at the
Lions. He is very sharp from a standing start out of dummy-half, and with
good hands. Paul be looking to force his way into first-team reckoning
during 2021.

SQUAD NUMBER : 24

Swinton Stats : Heritage Number 1299; **Appearances** 0; **Tries** 0.

PREVIOUS CLUBS Blackbrook ARLFC, St Helens

Autograph

JACOB SMILLIE

WINGER
D.O.B 16, September 1998
JOINED CLUB 01/12/2020

Jacob, a winger, came to the Lions late in 2020 from his hometown club Bradford Bulls. Prior to the Bulls he was emerging through the "A" team at Halifax, with whom he gained a reputation for scoring spectacular long-range tries with his blistering pace. The 21 year-old qualifies for Jamaica and will be looking to cement his place in the Reggae Warriors' squad for this year's World Cup. Jacob is another young player with great potential who fits our recruitment profile, and who could potentially go on to be a real star in the sport.

SQUAD NUMBER : 23

Swinton Stats : Heritage Number 0; **Appearances** 0; **Tries** 0.

PREVIOUS CLUBS Halifax, Bradford Bulls

Autograph

GERONIMO DOYLE

FULL-BACK / CENTRE / WINGER
D.O.B 6, January 1997
JOINED CLUB 01/12/2020

Geronimo spent a brief period training with the Lions early in 2020, but Covid-19 intervened before possible terms could be finalised. However, we were able to re-open our plans ahead of the 2021 season and secure his services. Geronimo is a New Zealander, who was previously with the Otahuhu Leopards in the Fox Memorial Premiership, the senior league in Auckland. The Kiwi, who turned 24 in January 2021, also has extensive experience playing representative rugby league in his own country, including appearances for the New Zealand Maori residents' team. Geronimo is a strong running, assured and well-balanced player, who can cover a variety of positions, including full-back, centre and wing. He is also a fine goal-kicker and is sure to become a firm crowd favourite.

SQUAD NUMBER : 22

Swinton Stats : Heritage Number 1298; **Appearances** 0; **Tries** 0.

PREVIOUS CLUBS Otahuhu Leopards (NZ)

Autograph

COBI GREEN

HALF-BACK
D.O.B 4, March 1999
JOINED CLUB 01/12/2020

Half-Back Cobi joined the Lions from Bradford Bulls ahead of the 2021 season. He entered the limelight late in 2019 when he was selected for Wales at the World Nines tournament in Sydney, and it was a chance he grasped with both hands as he produced some confident and polished performances. A former captain of the Wales under 19 side, Cobi shows all the hallmarks of a potential star in the making, and will be hoping to make the 2021 Welsh World Cup squad. Cobi is an exciting half-back with a high skill-set who is keen to take on the line and promote space for others.

SQUAD NUMBER : 18

Swinton Stats : Heritage Number 0; **Appearances** 0; **Tries** 0.

PREVIOUS CLUBS Bradford Bulls

Autograph

NICK GREGSON

SECOND-ROW
D.O.B 17, December 1995
JOINED CLUB 01/12/2020

Nick was another significant addition
to the Lions' squad ahead of the 2021
season. He will already be familiar to
Swinton fans having first made his
Lions debut back in 2016 whilst on
Dual Registration from Wigan. He
played twice more for Swinton in 2017,
then played in all 6 games at the back-end of the 2019 season whilst on loan
from Leigh Centurions – that being an impressive run that saw the Lions
gain crucial victories over Barrow, Halifax and Sheffield. Nick then looked
to try his hand at the Union code with Preston Grasshoppers, before
accepting this new opportunity with the Lions. He is an extremely versatile
player who will provide Stuart Littler with plenty of options.

SQUAD NUMBER : 12

Swinton Stats : Heritage Number 1222; **Appearances** 9; **Tries** 2.

PREVIOUS CLUBS Wigan Warriors, Leigh Centurions, Preston
Grasshoppers RUFC

Autograph

Behind the Scenes

Covid brought the 2020 season to a very abrupt end shortly after it had started. The Directors looked to bring some stability to the club and resigned the available players for 2021 season. A few of the squad left to join former colleagues elsewhere, but the bulk of the team remained loyal and resigned.

These were the 2020 Officials:

Board of Directors	Stephen Wild (CEO) Stuart Dickman Lindsey Smethills Stuart Fletcher Stephen Parker Barry McGuinness Damian Ridpath - Director of Development Paula Kenny - Non-Exec (Wellbeing)
Honorary President	David Jones
Head Coach	Stuart Littler
Assistant Coaches	Allan Coleman Dougie Owen
Performance Analyst	Chris Wharton
Strength & Conditioning	Colin Robinson
Physiotherapist	Lyndsey Watkins (Head) Norman Brown Sasha Cooke
Club Doctors	Dr Joe Amissah-Arthur Dr Rachel Leopold
Commercial Manager	Lindsey Smethills
Kitmen	Alan Gibbons (Head) Chris Gettins (Assistant)
Matchday Operations	Paul Leadbeater (Head of Security & Safety) John Holden (Ground Safety Officer & H&S Advisory) Alan Dixon (Time Keeper) Pete Green (Club Photographer) Emily Parker (Club Photographer) Colin Gettins (Match Day Financial Operations) Andy Daniels (PA Announcer) Colin James (Lions TV Camera) Stephen Johnson (Lions TV Camera) Chris Bell (Social Media and Website Editor) Helen Mather (Media Team) Harry Dunnett (Media Team)
Lottery Liaison Officer	Fred Dyson
Media Manager	Ian Rigg (Media Enquiries 07976 373561)
Programme Editor	Martin McDonough
Ambassador in North America	Geoff Hewitt

2021 Officials List

Board of Directors	Stuart Fletcher (Chairman) Stephen Wild (CEO) Damian Ridpath (Director of Development) Stuart Dickman Lindsey Smethills Stephen Parker Barry McGuinness Paula Kenny - Non-Exec (Wellbeing)
Honorary President	David Jones
Head Coach	Stuart Littler
Assistant Coaches	Allan Coleman Dougie Owen
Performance Analyst	Chris Wharton
Strength & Conditioning	Colin Robinson
Physiotherapist	Lyndsey Watkins (Head) Norman Brown Sasha Cooke
Club Doctor	Dr Joe Amissah-Arthur
Swinton Lionesses Head Coach	Martina Greenwood
Kitmen	Alan Gibbons (Head) Chris Gettins (Assistant)
Matchday Operations	Paul Leadbeater (Head of Security & Safety) John Holden (Ground Safety Officer & H&S Advisory) Alan Dixon (Time Keeper) Pete Green (Club Photographer) Emily Parker (Club Photographer) Colin Gettins (Match Day Financial Operations) Andy Daniels (PA Announcer) Colin James (Lions TV Camera) Stephen Johnson (Lions TV Camera) Sam Everall (Media Team) Helen Mather (Media Team) Harry Dunnett (Media Team)
Lottery Liaison Officer	Fred Dyson
Media Manager	Ian Rigg (Media Enquiries 07976 373561)
Programme Editor	Ian Jackson with Martin McDonough on Prog Creation
Ambassador in North America	Geoff Hewitt
Community Partner Clubs	FOLLY LANE ARLFC BELFAST EAGLES ARLFC DEVON SHARKS ARLFC LONGHORNS (DUBLIN) ARLFC KANO LIONS, NIGERIA
Cover Artwork	Katie Wild
Commercial Manager	Lindsey Smethills

2020

October

October's news was the signing of Jordan Brown from Widnes Vikings.
Jordan, who turned 20 last month, was born at Warrington, and came through the junior ranks at the Wolves before signing for our Championship rivals Widnes.

Jordan was thrilled to be joining the Lions. He said, "I'm made up to have been given the opportunity to sign for Swinton and I can't wait to knuckle down and meet the boys in pre-season.

"Then hopefully get my foot in the door with a first team place once play starts next year."

"WE SEE A LOT OF POTENTIAL FOR GROWTH AND DEVELOPMENT IN HIM"

Lions' Head Coach **Stuart Littler** believes that Jordan's capture could prove to be a very shrewd piece of business. He said, *"Our squad is really taking shape now and Jordan's signing adds to the competition for starting shirts.

"He is a good size athlete and can competently cover both the middle and back-row positions up front. Jordan has played in the academy and reserves at Widnes after being part of the Warrington scholarship scheme.

"We are really looking forward to getting to work with Jordan as we see a lot of potential in him.

"He's another highly promising young talent that meets our recruitment profile. Welcome to the Lions Jordan!"

November

Swinton were delighted to announce the appointment of Paula Kenny, who was to join the club in a non-executive director capacity.

Paula Kenny is a highly qualified psychotherapist in private practice, and in particular has extensive experience within the field of mental health.

Upon agreeing to assist the Lions **Paula** said, "I am very excited to be joining the Swinton Lions family and to be part of such a progressive organisation that is evidently extremely serious about supporting the wellbeing of its players, staff and supporters."

"The Lions' Operations Director Steve Wild added. "We are really thrilled that Paula has agreed to join our club in a non-executive management role. "The current pandemic is sufficient reminder, should it be needed, that many organisations, no matter what their field, need to step up to the plate in looking after the welfare of their most important commodity – its people. "We pride ourselves on being a family club as well as a professional club, and Paula's input will add another dimension to that philosophy. "Over the coming weeks and months Paula's experience and expertise will not just be available to everyone within our club family, but she also will be helping to drive some innovative programmes around welfare and mental health in the Swinton Lions name which will benefit the wider community."

Lionesses

The club was delighted to formally announce the appointment of former England international Martina Greenwood as the first ever Head Coach of the Swinton Lionesses!

Martina was joining us from Halifax Women's RLFC where she enjoyed immediate and substantial success.

We are thrilled that Martina has decided to join our organisation, and we feel sure that the Lionesses will soon emerge as a force in the sport under her leadership.
This important appointment follows the announcement back in March on International Women's Day, when our intention to launch a Swinton Lionesses team was first revealed.

The Covid crisis understandably then impacted on our intended timetable for the Lionesses, but we now plan to get our training programme back on track as from January 2021.
"I am now thrilled to be taking on this brand-new role at Swinton Lions with the Lionesses."

Upon her appointment **Martina** revealed, "I haven't always played rugby league, and in fact I came to the sport as a result of not being able to play Gaelic football competitively here in the UK.

"I started playing rugby league with the Bradford Thunderbirds at the age of 23, having never touched a rugby ball before. Things went well and two years later I was selected for the Yorkshire squad and I went on to represent the county for many seasons.

"I also went on to represent England Teachers as well as England "A", and I was a member of the full England squad before injuries caught up with me.

"During my rugby league playing journey I've also played in many Challenge Cup finals and League Championship finals. Some of these were won and some were lost, but always many a friend was made whilst I was playing.

"Off the pitch I have taken on numerous positions including club secretary, fixture secretary, and supporting many committees in a variety of roles! I have also been actively involved in coaching in both the male and female games and had many fabulous coaching and managing experiences.

"For instance, I toured Russia and France with the England under 21s squad and was Head Coach of the newly developed Girls' Super 4s Yorkshire programme. I was also identified by the RFL as a developing coach for their mentor programme.

"Having enjoyed coaching in junior set ups in both the male and female game, I then took the opportunity to become the first ever female Head Coach at Halifax RFLC Women's Team.

"I was then extremely proud when our Halifax team achieved promotion in its first season.

"However, I am now thrilled to be taking on this brand-new role at Swinton Lions with the Lionesses. I look forward to the new challenges ahead, and to developing the game of rugby league for women and girls in the Swinton and Manchester area."

"We are absolutely thrilled to be able to welcome Martina into the Swinton Lions Family."

Damian Ridpath, the Swinton Lions Director of Development, added, "We are delighted to have recruited Martina as Head Coach for the Lionesses.

"Once it was apparent that she was available we moved quickly to discuss our ambitions with Martina.

"We discovered that Martina shares a similar vision for the development of the female game, and we were absolutely thrilled to be able to welcome her into the Swinton Lions Family.

"Martina's track record is evident not just within a range of successful coaching posts, but she also has a tremendous insight as to how to develop and design pathways that will improve players of all abilities and ages.

"This wide-ranging knowledge and expertise, combined with Martina's leadership skills, will ensure our Women's and Girl's structure moving forward will be amongst the best rugby league has to offer."

The first Swinton Lionesses engagement day will take place on Sunday 17ᵗʰ January at 10am @ Folly Lane ARLFC, Blue Ribbon Field, Fraser Street, Pendlebury M27 4DH (female players with all levels of experience and abilities are welcome to come down and say hello!). There will be two age groups to begin with (16 to 18 years; along with open age), with further age groups to be announced in due course.

Swinton Lions, in association with community partner club Folly Lane, were also delighted to reveal that their newly formed women's team, the "Lionesses" will be based in both clubs' traditional hometown.

Back in March, ahead of the first national lockdown, Swinton Lions announced their intent to launch a Lionesses section.
Since then Covid has of course impacted on the intended timeframe, but behind the scenes positive conversations have continued with Folly Lane.

As a result of this partnership it can now be confirmed that the Lionesses will be based at Folly's Blue-Ribbon Field headquarters in Pendlebury, both for home matches as well as for training purposes.

The arrangement between the two organisations not only strengthens their community partnership, but it also means that a "Swinton" named rugby league team will be playing in the town after an absence of some 28 years. The Lionesses project also represents a major step-forward for the development of female rugby league in the Swinton, Salford and Greater Manchester area.
"It's a great opportunity for both of our clubs!"
Folly Lane's **Gary Woodward** was delighted with this latest development in the relationship between his club and Swinton Lions. He said "Folly Lane are excited to be hosting The Lionesses in 2021.
"It's a great opportunity for both of our clubs. I'm sure that supporters of both Swinton and Folly will get behind this.
"The standard of women's RL has improved massively since the days of Folly Lane running a team over 20 years ago, and it's only going to get better.
"Our club will open to all, so come down, watch the game, have a drink, a bite to eat, and enjoy the match. Good luck Lionesses!"
"Folly is a fantastic club and one that I have a special affinity for!"

The Lionesses Head Coach **Martina Greenwood**, added, "I'm delighted that the Lionesses will be based in our traditional hometown.

"Folly is a fantastic club and one that I have a special affinity for, particularly as both my son and brother are playing members.

"I'd encourage all prospective players, regardless of ability or experience, to come down and give our great sport a try.

"Aside from keeping fit and learning new skills, you'll be sure to make lots of friends."

Damian Ridpath, the Swinton Lions Director of Development, was equally enthusiastic. He enthused, "On behalf of Swinton Lions I want to thank Gary Woodward and everyone at Folly Lane for so readily buying into our vision for the women's game in the Swinton and Manchester area.

"Our intention is to field an open-age side during 2021, as well as a 16 to 18 years team.

"The important thing is for girls and women to come down and have a go at the sport.

"In Martina we have recruited an outstanding coach, and our Lionesses will be sure to progress from strength to strength."

LIONS CONFIRM CHAIRMAN
Swinton Lions have continued the process of revamping their off-field structure with the appointment of Stuart Fletcher as their new club Chairman.

Stuart Fletcher became a Director a year ago at the invitation of Operations Director Steve Wild, who was then in the process of assembling a new Board.

Stuart had previously been a regular sponsor and club benefactor, as well as being a life-long fan of the Lions and rugby league in general.

In his new position Stuart will draw on a wide variety of experiences from his professional background as a senior officer in a government law department.

The Lions' Operations Director Steve Wild explained, "When I began the process of assembling a new management structure a year ago, Stuart's name was the first on my list of people to approach.

"He is someone I trust implicitly, and not just because he is a personal friend.

"Stuart will bring great pride as well as significant value to the post.

"Professionally he has an impressive CV having worked with some extremely senior people at the highest level. He is a peoples' person, yet very astute and analytical.

"But most of all he loves Swinton Lions to the core, and I know he will give everything to the role of Chairman.

"This appointment represents another significant piece of our development jigsaw."

"I feel so proud to be able to lead the Lions on this exciting journey!"

Upon accepting the role **Stuart** said, "It is a great honour to be appointed Chairman of our historic club.

"I attended my first Swinton game in 1969 and feel so proud to be able to lead the Lions on this exciting journey as we establish ourselves as a positive, outward looking club within the rugby league community.

"I do not take lightly the responsibility that comes with the role. I can assure everyone connected with Swinton Lions that I am 100% committed to the growth of the club and to building on our great history and heritage.

"It is a privilege to be Chairman when we have a Board of Directors comprising of dedicated, highly skilled individuals who lead from the front.

"We also have tremendous players, coaching team, backroom staff, and volunteers – plus not forgetting our fantastic supporters who I firmly believe are the most loyal in rugby league.

"The game is changing on and off the field and I will ensure that we are not complacent, but rather in a strong position to meet the challenges ahead.

"We are currently in the middle of a significant process of engagement with the RFL, our governing body, through which we intend to outline our strategic vision.

"Our intention is to demonstrate to the rugby league community that Swinton Lions is a club with significant ambition.

"This marvellous club belongs to us all and as Chairman I want to be seen as approachable and transparent.

"The role also requires decisive decision making, and clarity in communications, and so it's appropriate that our stakeholders understand decisions that affect the club.

"Finally, on behalf of the whole Board, I'd like to thank our superb loyal fans and club partners for your ongoing support. In the meantime, especially in this unprecedented period of worldwide uncertainty, please keep safe."

December

1ˢᵗ December and preseason training recommenced.

On 6ᵗʰ December the club released their shirt designs for the forthcoming season.

Appropriately in Rugby League World Cup year, our 2021 principle playing colours for both our Lions and newly formed Lionesses pays homage to the traditional Swinton Lions shirt which recently won the Rugby League's prestigious World Cup of kits tournament on Twitter.

Designed by our team wear partners **SuPro,** our blue jersey with the instantly recognisable white "V" is of course iconic in the eyes of Lions supporters.

The royal blue top with white "V" first saw the light of day at the Lancashire Cup Final of 29th October 1960 and soon saw back-to-back Championship successes in 1963 and 1964, but 60 years later it is still the kit which most resonates with the Swinton name across the world of rugby league football.

The OFFICIAL most iconic kit in the history of the British game will therefore no doubt prove to be a big hit with Lions followers, who will be eagerly looking forward to getting back on the terraces following the enormous challenges we've all faced over the past year.

We'd also like to take this opportunity to pay a special thank you to each of our proud sponsors and club partners, each of whom features on the new shirt:-

Our headline club sponsor is now **GLOSSOP CARAVAN**S, whose logo is emblazoned across the front of the new design.

On the chest we also have the **WHITE SWAN HOTEL** of Swinton, and up on the collars **CAMWAY INSTALLATIONS**.

On the sleeves we feature **ADVANCED STEEL SERVICES, TITAN STEEL**, and our official travel partners **SWAN'S TRAVEL**.

On the reverse **DAISYMILL TECHNOLOGIES** will sit proudly above the player number, and beneath it we feature the logo of the magnificently successful supporter led organisation, PRIDE BUILDER.

The choice of gold and red for our secondary kit is a deliberate celebration of the principal colours of the official Coat of Arms of Swinton and Pendlebury, which itself is featured in shadow on the front of the shirt.

The Borough's Coat of Arms was first introduced in September 1934 alongside the town's Royal Charter, at the start of a season which culminated in Swinton Lions being crowned champions of England for a fourth time.

A shield featuring a gold cockatrice, beneath a red lion passant and two red roses of Lancashire, is flanked by two rampant golden lions.

The red and gold Coat of Arms is topped by a Swinton boar's head, all of which rides above the legend "Salus Populi Suprema Lex" – the welfare of the people is the highest law! An appropriate slogan with which to salute the dedication of our loyal fans.

This fresh and exciting kit is a nod to the modern era, but it is not without historical significance!

KIWI GERONIMO JOINS THE LIONS!
16 December 2020

Swinton announced the signing of Geronimo Doyle, a New Zealander, who was previously with the Otahuhu Leopards in the Fox Memorial Premiership, the senior league in Auckland.

The Kiwi, who will turn 24 in January, also has extensive experience playing representative rugby league in his own country, including appearances for the New Zealand Maori residents' team.

Geronimo is a strong running and well-balanced player, who can cover a variety of positions, including full-back, centre and wing. He is also a fine goal-kicker.
"I can't wait to meet the entire Lions family"

Upon signing for the Lions, Geronimo said, "I'm really excited to be joining Swinton Lions for the 2021 season.

"I've heard a lot about the club's strong tradition and history in the sport.

"I've also heard about the team's loyal supporters, and I can't wait to meet the entire Lions family.

"The Lions have remained busy throughout Covid and have been building towards the new season, and I hope my addition to the squad will assist in taking the team forward."

Head Coach Stuart Littler added, "We are delighted to have been able to secure Geronimo's signature after competing with other Championship clubs to get this deal done.

"Geronimo trained with us as a guest pre-Covid and he looked very accomplished within our set-up.

"He is certainly an exciting talent and he is someone who I feel can add real value to our squad and substantially increase competition for places.

"Geronimo can cover a whole host of positions in the backs and he tells me he is really excited by the potential and future we can offer.

"I'm sure you will all welcome Geronimo, as he definitely has all the attributes to become a firm crowd favourite."

Once again, the Club would like to acknowledge Pride Builder and the generosity of its members for their vital input in making this deal happen.

BRANDON WOOD TO CONCENTRATE ON BUSINESS INTERESTS
17 December 2020

Swinton Lions and Brandon Wood have reached a compromise agreement which will enable the winger to concentrate on outside business commitments.

Brandon won't be available to train or play for the foreseeable future, but the Lions have left the door open should circumstances change at any point during 2021.

Brandon had joined the club ahead of the ill-fated 2020 season, and played in all of Swinton's five competitive games before the lockdown

2021

January

RL WORLD CUP LEGACY GRANT FOR LIONS' FOUNDATION'S JOSE KENGA PROJECT!

6th January 2021

Swinton Lions Community Sports Foundation received £2738.96 from the CreatedBy RLWC2021 Capital Grants Legacy Programme!

The grant, which has been awarded to help more people play rugby league at grassroots level in Greater Manchester, will fund the club's new Jose Kenga Diversity and Inclusion Project.

Swinton Lions Community Sports Foundation is set to receive £2738.96 from the CreatedBy RLWC2021 Capital Grants Programme.

Delivered in partnership between RLWC2021, the sport's national governing body, the Rugby Football League, Sport England and the Department for Digital, Culture, Media & Sport, the CreatedBy programme is a funding pot of up to £10million made available by the government to support the legacy of the Rugby League World Cup by growing participation in the sport.

The funding will be used to facilitate a bespoke activity programme within the City of Salford and Borough of Trafford. It will provide participants a Diversity and Inclusion Workshop combined alongside a Rugby League playing opportunity across six Greater Manchester locations.

Damian Ridpath, Director of Development for the Swinton Lions Community Sports Foundation, said: "We are absolutely delighted to receive this funding.

"Inspired by one of our key players, Jose Kenga, who was born in the Democratic Republic of Congo, it will facilitate an innovative programme which combines a bespoke workshop for young people linked with rugby league playing activities.

"The programme will also act as a catalyst for forming new community teams for both boys and girls and assist in the capturing new recruits for the next generation of young Lions.

"As the only professional team whose match day operations are based in the same borough as the World Cup Final itself, it is important to ensure that we provide a legacy for our sport within the Borough of Trafford, as well as providing opportunities within our historical hometown of Swinton."

Jon Dutton, Chief Executive, RLWC2021, said: "The CreatedBy RLWC2021 Capital Grants Programme is focused on ensuring the next generation of rugby league players have the best possible experience and barriers to participate are removed.
"We are delighted to award this grant to Swinton Lions Community Sports Foundation and look forward to seeing the results of this investment that aims to deliver real change in their community."
Ralph Rimmer, Chief Executive of the Rugby Football League, said: "Hosting the Rugby League World Cup in 2021 offers so many opportunities for everyone involved in the game in this country and beyond, and the facilities that will be delivered by the CreatedBy RLWC2021 Capital Grants Programme will be a big part of that transformation.
"The RFL are proud to be involved in that process, and we congratulate all the successful applicants – and look forward to the impact of this unprecedented level of investment in the game for years to come."
Charles Johnston, Property Director, Sport England, said: "We are proud to be working in partnership to deliver the biggest government investment into grassroots rugby league facilities the country has ever seen.

"With this funding, communities will gain better access to the facilities, improved infrastructure and essential equipment they need to be active.
"We are pleased the investment will provide benefit to people engaging in the men's, women's and wheelchair game, with a focus on those disadvantaged areas where inactivity levels are stubbornly high.
"By focusing our efforts on increasing participation in the game, we're ensuring that the Rugby League World Cup's legacy lasts long after the last ball has been kicked and the crowds have gone home."

The Rugby League World Cup 2021 will kick off on 23 October 2021, with the men's, women's and wheelchair competitions taking place simultaneously, under one tournament banner for the first time.

LIONS MOURN LOSS OF DAVE NICHOLSON
25ᵗʰ January
The club announced the sad news on the sudden passing of former player,
Dave Nicholson.

Dave, a strong running
second row, joined the
Lions from
Blackbrook ARLFC
after returning from
the pioneering
BARLA Open Age
Tour of Papua New
Guinea, Australia and
New Zealand. Folly Lane's Bernard Southern was a teammate on that Tour.

Dave made his debut for the Lions in September 1979 and went on to play a
total of 31 games and score 8 tries, before Frank Myler took Dave and Alan
Taylor to Oldham at the end of the 1980/81 season.

One of the most popular of players and the nicest lad you could wish to
meet, Dave had lived on the Isle of Man for many years where he continued
his hobby of breeding canaries.

Dave's passing is indeed a terrible shock, but for all of us who knew him on
both sides of the touchline, it has been a true privilege to have shared a part
of his life.

Our hearts go out to Lesley, Joyce, Geri and family at this sad, sad time. God
Bless you Dave, RIP.

We are grateful to Steve Moyse for providing these words.

27ᵗʰ January
Covid was still proving to be an issue and another lockdown was ordered by
the UK Government which also impacted the start of the 2021 season. As a
result, the club announced:

"The actual 2020 printed Season Tickets would be distributed to those
supporters who donated the cost. These tickets will then double-up as "1866
Club" Memberships Cards during the 2021 season. Membership benefits are
likely to be influenced by the Covid-19 situation, so further details will

follow in due course. Entry to games will be on a simple match-by-match basis, with an online pre-purchase ticket facility available via the club website."

Steve Wild commented
"The Biggest challenge at present is Return to Train and Return to Play and ensuring compliance with DCMS /RFL COVID-19 protocol."

"We should have returned to train in November but that was delayed until 1st December; then the post Xmas resumption was temporarily delayed owing to lockdown 2. We recommenced last week, but under strict controls as to who can attend; and what we can actually do. We are regarded as an "elite club", hence we received clearance to train."

Rhodri Lloyd added:

We began training on the 3rd of December and have trained Tuesday and Thursdays until the end of the year of 2020. We were due to stray back on the 2nd of January. However, we were cut short obviously because of the new government lockdown. We resumed training the week commencing the 17th of January.

Firstly, I was quite anxious about starting training, but the club have done a fantastic job in keeping us all safe. The club have made sure we are tested regularly twice a week; our temperatures are being done regularly and we are in small training groups. I believe all that the lads were similar to myself, but then having seen what we have in place they were all at ease.

As a group we are just trying to get as much training as possible to prepare for the forthcoming season, it has been difficult because we are restricted in a lot of areas. Who knows what is going to happen, we as a group are aiming for the end of March start, but we expect some form of adjustment if COVID cases don't improve? We are an adaptable group, and we are prepared for whatever the future holds. At the end of the day, we just want to play rugby.

LIONS THRILLED WITH ANALYSIS PRO!

02 February 2021

Head Coach Stuart Littler reviews the impact of the club's new performance analysis tools.

At Swinton Lions, we chose to partner with AnalysisPro to supply the club's performance analysis tools in preparation for the upcoming 2021 season!

We are a part-time professional Championship Rugby League club, so we have to ensure we operate within sensible budgets, but also meet specific time frames regarding accessibility to players due to their work commitments and the balance of everyday family life. 2020 was of course an exceptional year, and one in which the season was cancelled for the first time in our lifetimes.

I have personally used the Nacsport video analysis software in collaboration with AnalysisPro to assist with coaching strategies throughout my time at Swinton as Head Coach. I have found Nacsport to be a leading performer in the video analysis field.

At the end of every season our Performance Staff sit down to review what has gone well, but to also ask the question, "How can we be even better?"

That review is structured so that each department within our performance team gets the opportunity to study the impact from tailored strategies, but also gets the opportunity to suggest how we can make things better. As a club, we are constantly assessing where we are at, but also how we can improve things to make Swinton the best learning environment and the most professional organisation it can be.

Within our latest annual review, our performance team highlighted that our performance analysis tools could be more efficient and effective – hence our decision to partner with AnalysisPro. In this release, I will discuss our intentions for each of the performance tools, and later in the year I will provide an update to discuss specifics within our performance analysis system and its impact upon the team's performance.

I'd also like to stress that we had the full support of our Board at Swinton, together with the Supporters' Trust, to acquire our new tools.

First up, we purchased two additional Nacsport Basic licences that are intended for use by my assistant coach Allan Coleman and our lead analyst Chris Wharton. By moving us all to the Nacsport platform, our video analysis will run from the same systems, making it easier for players to understand, whilst also making video sharing and editing between staff easier to complete. When analysing any video or forming new structures/specifics, we try to make things as simple as possible to promote clarity and understanding within our group. Nacsport now allows us to complete all our individual reviews, all the team previews and reviews, as well as allowing the coaching team to utilise videos that support the understanding of any given role within our team. More Nacsport licences have also given us more eyes in forming game plans and assessing opposition structures. The more ideas and discussion points we can formulate, the better our detail when given to our playing staff in supporting upcoming performances. We have found Nacsport to be a leading performer within this sector.

As well as access to Nacsport, I also had a play around pre-lockdown with the KlipDraw Animate tool, which integrates with Nacsport and allows us to draw or highlight specific areas within our video analysis, to improve the understanding of the processes involved in any targeted area of performance. KlipDraw was available for a trial period, so I utilised the offer and found that the support videos were great in getting up to speed with best practice to optimise performance. After this trial period, we decided that our videos would have greater impact with this tool, as well as allowing us to highlight specific scenarios that again promoted greater understanding within our playing group.

Lastly on the video analysis side, we had previously emailed individual information out, and team previews and reviews were completed in meeting rooms at our training venues. Again, with Covid related implications as well as our player accessibility, we wanted to create a classroom that was available to our players 24/7, as all our players have varying work schedules. By linking with the Sharimg platform, we have transferred our Video Learning Room to a cloud area, which enables our players to have 24/7 access to video reviews, previews of both game days, but also to training scenarios and discussion points. By using the Sharimg platform, we are ensuring our footage is easily accessible to our players who can access it from their phones, tablets or computers and smart TV's.

Away from the video analysis, discussions between our Head Coach and Lead Strength & Conditioner led to the suggestion that some GPS performance systems would support the 'challenge aspect' within our team dynamics in training, but it would also give us a performance tool that could be used to gain access to hard data, including kilometres covered, impacts, sprints, hard running efforts as well  as top speeds throughout individual and team performances. We therefore chose the SPT GPS system from AnalysisPro to answer this requirement.

SPT has been very useful for us to support data driven decision making, which supports our wellbeing screens, testing and the coaching team's opinions. The SPT Gametraka platform allows us to share this data with the team as soon as it's uploaded. This data is freely available to our players across all devices and in turn has generated some further competition elements within our squad. We are looking forward to utilising the tools in games at the start of the upcoming season. This data will allow us to be proactive rather than reactive in our decision-making process on individual players, but also on team decisions when aiming to periodise training schedules to optimise our team's performance levels throughout 2021.

As a performance team, we are delighted with the current impact from all the new tools we have purchased from AnalysisPro. The support from all the partners involved is second to none and any minor issues have been cleared up with both speed and efficiency. We will be in touch later in the year to evaluate the impacts of each of our analysis tools, as we expect each to improve player interactions as the season draws closer.

Stuart Littler, Swinton Lions Head Coach.

MORE GREAT BACKING FROM LIONS FANS!
05 February 2021
Swinton Lions have confirmed record player sponsorship income as their preparations for the 2021 season continue at pace!

Operations Director Steve Wild explains, "With the impact of Covid-19 creating other priorities, we were a bit later than usual this year in looking to attract player sponsors.
"Therefore, it was just a week ago today, that we began the process inviting pre-existing sponsors the opportunity to renew. We then extended the net to the wider fan base, and all I can say is that the response has been absolutely astonishing!
"We offered an ambitious looking 83 separate individual sponsorship packages at a range of prices, but in less than a week the whole lot had been sold out.
"Our sales figures in this specific area are up over 30% on our previous record and bearing in mind the fact that our fans and partners haven't seen a game for nearly 12 months, and we're still in the middle of a terrible

pandemic which has affected so many lives, we are absolutely humbled by the response.

"Perhaps it should come as no surprise, given the ongoing and tremendous efforts of our supporter groups such as Pride Builder, The Supporters Trust, and the Station Roaders. So, from everyone at the club, including of course all of our fully sponsored players, a massive thank you to all concerned. Pound for pound Swinton Lions fans are the best in the sport bar none."

14th February 2021
2021 BETFRED CHAMPIONSHIP FIXTURES ANNOUNCED !

Following a whole year out of action, the Lions will soon be back on the field in the BetFred Championship!

On the opening day of the 2021 season, Swinton will have a mouth-watering local derby against Oldham at Bower Fold on Good Friday.

The Lions' first league game at Heywood Road will be against Featherstone Rovers on Sunday 18th April, which will be followed a week later by the visit of York.

Owing to the restricted length of the season, four games are excluded from the calendar. The "missing" games being trips to Featherstone and newly promoted Newcastle Thunder, together with home games against Toulouse and Whitehaven.

Ahead of the opening league fixtures, the Lions will of course start their season with a home cup-tie on Sunday 21st March against Newcastle Thunder. Should Swinton be successful in that game, they will welcome the winners of the Oldham versus Barrow tie a week later. Both of these rounds will double-up as both Challenge Cup and 1895 Cup ties.

Current indications are that the early part of the season (at minimum) will be played behind closed doors, and considerable work is going on behind the scenes with our stadium partners Sale FC to ensure that Heywood Road is

Covid protocol compliant. However, it is hoped that any behind closed doors matches will be available to view via the "Our League" app.

25ᵗʰ February 2021

The website *Seriousaboutrl.Com* wrote an article on their predictions for the forthcoming season. This was their prediction for the Swinton Lions:

They certainly know how to survive and adapt and there is no reason why Swinton are unable to do so once again. Having survived relegation since their admission in 2016, as well as overcoming their financial difficulties off-field, Swinton are back for more in 2021. Under Stuart Littler, they possess experienced players in Martyn Ridyard, Mike Butt, Jack Hansen and captain Will Hope. Though they look rather inexperienced in depth, no doubt they will all be hungry for action and could very well cause an upset or two heading forward.
Prediction: 11th

Rhodri was the captain and not Will, so the facts were incorrect.

March
THE LIONS ARE BACK AT HEYWOOD ROAD!
01 March 2021

After exactly one year and one week, the Lions finally returned to the Heywood Road turf at the weekend!

Against the backdrop of a full-scale training exercise, the Lions fielded their full 2021 squad in an internal Blues versus Whites game consisting of three periods of 25 minutes.

Head Coach Stuart Littler was delighted to see his team back on the field. He said "It was great to be back doing what we all love to do. The sun was shining, and today's session proved there is light at the end of the tunnel. We can now have huge optimism about the future in front of us.

"Everything ran smoothly, and it was great to see the boys back out in some in-house competitive action, even it was just a training exercise. We now move into a game week scenario with footage to review and stats to compile, but most of all with opposition to prepare for!

"We will assess the learning points from the exercise and move forward together. Massive credit must go to our medical team and Board who are ensuring that we meet all of the extensive Covid protocol, so that we create an environment that is as safe as possible for all of our playing squad and staff."

Operations Director Steve Wild added, "It's been a long and complicated road to get to the stage where we could hold the training exercise yesterday, but it couldn't have happened without the enthusiasm and professionalism of all our staff and volunteers. We have also had tremendous support from our friends at Sale FC, who already possess the invaluable experience of playing Behind Closed Doors games at Heywood Road.
"The exercise at the weekend was not just a significant step-forward for Stuart and his players and staff in preparing for a full return to action, it was also a key off-field exercise as we prepare for our first Behind Closed Doors action against Newcastle Thunder on 21

March. The Covid rules and regulations are understandably lengthy and complex, so therefore to have a dry run was extremely useful. Happily, the day went well both on and off the pitch, with no major glitches.
"It was fantastic to see the lads out on the pitch after such a long and enforced break, and hopefully it won't be too long before we can open the gates and welcome back all of our friends and partners."

LIONS DEFEAT BRADFORD ON LONG-AWAITED RETURN!
07 March 2021
The Lions put in a stunning performance to claim victory against the Bulls in a cold and sunny afternoon in Dewsbury.

Bradford Bulls 22-26 Swinton Lions
It was a great opportunity for Stuart Littler and John Kear to look at both their squads in a full-blown match and there was some really good talent on show. Bradford went with a squad of twenty-seven which included three trialists and the Lions had twenty-four players in their squad.

The Bulls took the lead in the fourth minute when the Lions were on the attack but a kick towards the line for the chasers was collected by Matty Dawson Jones who broke downfield before passing the ball on to the supporting Brandon Pickersgill who scored under the posts and Danny Brough added the simple conversion.

The Lions then tried to hit back quickly when Martyn Ridyard kicked a forty-twenty, but the ball was lost in the second tackle and the chance went. Bulls started to press the line again but there was some excellent defence on

show when firstly George Flanagan was held up over the line by Nick Gregson and a few minutes later Ross Oakes looked like he might score but Richard Lepori and Liam Forsyth managed to hold him up too and the chance went.

The Lions started to fight back and forced a goal line drop out and from the kick Mitch Cox went close on the left only to be knocked into touch by Pickersgill. Bulls scrum half Jordan Lilley was dispatched to the sin bin by referee Jack Smith in the twenty-second minute for an off the ball challenge on Jack Hansen. From the resulting penalty the Lions had more pressure on the Bulls line, and it looked like Luke Waterworth might score but he lost control of the ball reaching for the try line. Bulls then added a second try a few minutes later when Oakes broke a couple of tackles to score on the left and Brough again converted.

The Lions were still chipping at the Bulls defence and just before the break Rhodri Lloyd broke through on the right to feed the supporting Jack Hansen and he raced in to score and Ridyard added the conversion but in the build up to the try Jose Kenga got a leg injury and had to leave the field having come on as a substitute ninety seconds earlier.

The Bulls started the second half the same way as they started the first capitalising on a Lions handling error and Dawson Jones scored in the left corner and Billy Jowitt added the conversion from the touchline. Again, the Lions were on the attack and Mike Butt scored in the left corner after some good build up play by Ridyard and Geronimo Doyle down the left but the conversion from Ridyard hit the posts and bounced away, but they were just eight points behind ten minutes into the second half.

Five minutes later and the Lions were in for another try when this time Hansen broke the Bulls defence to feed Doyle who raced away to score on the left and this time the conversion was good from Ridyard. Another three minutes passed, and another try from the Lions when the impressive Deane Meadows dummied and twisted his way to the line to score and again a good conversion from Ridyard found the Lions four points ahead at the midway point of the second half. The Bulls were not finished and on sixty-three minutes Flanagan darted over from short range but somehow Jowitt managed to miss from in front of the posts and the scores were locked at twenty-two all. Bulls trialist Brad Calland tried to win the game for his side with eight minutes left when he attempted a drop goal, but it sailed wide.

Rhodri Lloyd scored the winning try with six minutes left when he went over in the left corner and with Ridyard having a deserved rest on the bench the touchline conversion attempt from Hansen struck the left post and bounced out but the Bulls could not get past the Lions defence in the final minutes and victory was claimed.

Ian Rigg at The Tetley's Stadium

Teams:
BULLS – Pickersgill, Brown, Hamlett, Oakes, Dawson Jones, Brough, Lilley, Walker, Flanagan, Crossley, Gallagher, England, Fleming. SUBS: Scurr, Doyle, Nzoungo, Foggin-Johnston, Wallis, Jowitt, Ho, Berry, M Smith, O'Hanlon, S Smith, Calland, Burton, Rooks.
Tries: Pickersgill, Oakes, Dawson Jones, Flanagan
Goals: Brough 2, Jowitt 1

LIONS– Butt, Lepori, Cox, Forsyth, Doyle, Ridyard, Hansen, Brooks, Waterworth, Hatton, Lloyd, Gregson, Brogan. SUBS: Brickhill, Green, Jones, Meadows, Grant, T Brown, Roberts, Heyes, Nash, Kenga, J Brown.
Tries: Hansen, Butt, Doyle, Meadows, Lloyd
Goals: Ridyard 3
Referee: Jack Smith

JOSE KENGA INJURY SETBACK FOR LIONS

11 March 2021

Last Saturday the Lions launched their post-Covid comeback with an encouraging 26-22 victory away to Bradford Bulls, but unfortunately the positive mood from that friendly success has suffered a subsequent setback.

Swinton forward Jose Kenga had entered the field as a first-half substitute, but within less than 2 minutes he was forced off the field with what looked like a lower leg injury. Jose subsequently attended hospital where sadly a ruptured Achilles was diagnosed. This type of injury has the potential to side-line Jose for several months, which of course is a devastating blow to the player and the club.

Head Coach Stuart Littler lamented the loss of this popular member of his squad. He said, "Sadly it's not great news from the hospital regarding the injury to Jose. There is always a risk in any rugby match of a player getting injured due to contact and the physical elements of the game. But to be fair in this case, having looked back at the video, it's hard to determine what actually went wrong.

"We have been in constant contact with Jose since last Saturday and we have already started to formulate a rehab programme to get him back up and running. Jose will now focus on getting his recovery right with our medical team who have been outstanding throughout pre-season.

"Things are sometimes sent to test us. But by focussing on the positives, it allows us to build resilience to adversity in challenging times. We are a close team, and we will all support Jose to get back on that field as soon as possible."

Over the last few days, the club has received a number of enquiries and messages in respect of Jose's well-being. Jose thanks everyone for their support and is determined to return to action as soon as physically possible. In the meantime, the club's internal support systems will be focussing on his welfare and recovery.

BERNARD SCOTT – AN OBITUARY
16 March 2021

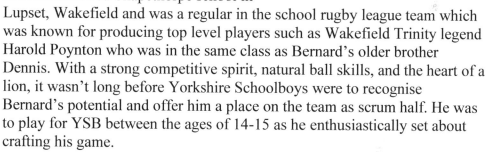

We have been greatly saddened to learn of the death at the weekend of our former prop-forward Bernard Scott, and on behalf of everyone associated with Swinton RLFC, we would like to pass on our heartfelt condolences to Bernard's family and many friends.

We are indebted to Bernard's nephew, Tom Scott, for the following magnificent summary of his uncle's career in rugby league:-

SCHOOLBOY RUGBY
Bernard attended Snapethorpe school in Lupset, Wakefield and was a regular in the school rugby league team which was known for producing top level players such as Wakefield Trinity legend Harold Poynton who was in the same class as Bernard's older brother Dennis. With a strong competitive spirit, natural ball skills, and the heart of a lion, it wasn't long before Yorkshire Schoolboys were to recognise Bernard's potential and offer him a place on the team as scrum half. He was to play for YSB between the ages of 14-15 as he enthusiastically set about crafting his game.

SHAW CROSS BOYS CLUB
Bernard joined Shaw Cross Boys Club in 1957 and quickly became a key player at the local amateur club which was renowned for producing a steady stream of talented players. Scouts from numerous professional teams were always in attendance at Shaw Cross in search of the future stars of the game and this is where his first professional club, Halifax RLFC picked up his services in 1961 when he was aged 19. This was the break that Bernard was looking for and an opportunity to show his skills at the highest levels of the game.

HALIFAX RLFC – Heritage Number 717
Bernard joined the club from Shaw Cross in 1961 and stayed until 1966. Several other players signed from Shaw Cross around that time, including Barney Hardcastle, Stuart Kelley, Barrie Cooper, and Trevor Stevenson. His signing-on fee was £500. They came to training together every Tuesday and Thursday night on a minibus that the club put on for them. They all became

very good friends. During his playing career at Halifax he made 65 appearances in total, all at prop, scoring 5 tries. His debut was on 30th September, 1961, at Hull KR, soon after signing. It was notable that this was also the debut game of a 17 year old Colin Dixon who had joined from Welsh Rugby Union. His last match was at Keighley on 3rd September, 1966. Bernard played at the same time as fellow-greats of the game Ken Roberts, and Jack Scroby. Halifax were one of the top sides in the period, winning several trophies. Bernard was in the team for the final of the Eastern Region competition in 1965, a long-defunct yet very significant competition. Bernard played in the 1964/65 championship winning side and although he missed out on the championship final, equivalent of the current Grand Final. He was to play in most of the earlier rounds.

He loved his playing days at Halifax and formed a strong bond with the many elite players that performed for the club in one of its greatest eras in the early sixties. He was proud to have played alongside Colin Dixon and Terry Michael who had both joined Halifax to gain opportunities that were not available to them in those times in Welsh Rugby Union. They became good friends and Colin was made welcome at the family home in Wakefield on many occasions. Bernard's reputation as a tough, uncompromising prop with excellent ball handling skills attracted the interest of Swinton in 1966 when they made a very substantial offer of £2000 for his services. He did not really want to leave, but the Halifax board of directors had decided the offer was too much to refuse at a time when finances were beginning to come under pressure. He met his wife to be, June, during his time at Halifax and he always looked back on this period of his playing career with great fondness. He continued to meet up with his pals at the many players reunions that he attended long after his playing career ended.

SWINTON RLFC – Heritage Number 546
Bernard Scott was in the prime of his career when he signed for the Lions in 1966 from Halifax for the large fee of £2000 (equivalent of about £37500 in today's money). He made his debut on 9th September 1966 in a 25-4 win at Widnes, when he also scored a try. In all, he made 93 first team appearances for the club and scored 5 tries. One of the most prestigious games he played in for Swinton was against Castleford in the final of the 1966 BBC2 Floodlit Cup, which Swinton were to lose 7-2. It should be noted that during this period Bernard had a young family back at home in Ossett and he worked during the day as an engineer. Travelling across the Pennines in those days for training on an evening and game days, before the M62 had been built, was a remarkable dedication to one of the toughest sports on earth. Typically, Bernard was manfully up to the challenge! As it was so difficult

and not always possible to travel to away games in these times for both players and fans, the players would also play regularly in the "A" team in a home fixture and these teams were therefore perhaps much stronger than the teams of today. During the 60's "A" team fixtures were highly

competitive and commanded big crowds. Bernard continued to perform at the highest level throughout his career at Station Road until knee injuries began to take their toll and he finally retired from top level rugby league in 1972. However, he would continue his passion for the game by playing and being involved with his hometown amateur club of Ossett. Bernard played for 6 years at the club in his specialist position as prop before finally retiring in 1972 having had a long and successful playing career.

The joint records provided by Halifax and Swinton club historians show that Bernard made a total of 158 first team appearances with most, if not all, in the very toughest of positions as prop forward. Participating in the most uncompromising and challenging of sports, Bernard faced up to some of the hardest men ever to play the great game of rugby league.

CHAIRMAN'S MESSAGE
20 March 2021
With the season upon us I am sure everyone connected with the Lions is eagerly awaiting the start of what promises to be an exciting journey and glad to be back playing after what has been a traumatic past year.

The performance at Bradford Bulls in the pre-season friendly showed what this club is all about – character and determination to clinch a deserved victory. The victory was marred by the devastating injury to Jose and the club fully supports Jose in his recovery programme. Jose has stated he will come back stronger and in the meantime he will be involved in many off-field Lions' initiatives.

There are various groups to say a big thank you following the past year, which to say has been challenging for the club would be understatement.

I have stated previously our supporters are the best in the league and I truly believe that with the various adversities that the club has faced and overcome yet we continue grow stronger and stronger. The significant financial donations through 2020 season tickets plus the superb work of the Supporters Trust and Pride Builder are pivotal to our growth on and off the field so thank you.

In such an unstable period I say a big thank you to our business partners who continue to support the club with valued sponsorship. I look forward to working closely with our sponsors as we continue to grow.

Our playing, coaching, backroom staff were faced with the uncertainty of when we would be returning to train and play, but the professionalism of everyone in ensuring fitness was maintained emphasised the dedication and commitment of our staff so a big thank you.

The work needed to meet Covid protocols, firstly to return to training and then to get sign off to play behind closed doors has been a minefield. This has resulted in many, many long days, nights, weekends by so many people to ensure we get sign off by the RFL and local authority to get to the place where this Sunday can take place. My personal gratitude to all concerned. This has not been straightforward.

I just want to say how the RFL have supported all clubs in getting season 2021 up and running and in the many meetings we have had it is obvious our governing body is held in high esteem by the Government and has represented our sport effectively.
Our community work continues to grow and we have close partnerships with our partner clubs Folly Lane, Belfast Eagles, Devon Sharks, Longhorns and the Kano Lions, with the Lions supporting each club in their development. Work continues in various different strands of community engagement so watch out for more news on this front.

The Lionesses are an integral part of the club and the commitment and enthusiasm of all concerned is fantastic to see led by Head Coach Martina and it will be emotional and exciting to see the Lionesses start playing in our famous kit up at Folly Lane.

The club is in a solid position on and off the field with professionalism in every aspect of what we do. This is evidenced by the purchase of state of the art software for training analysis and the development of our own club gym at the AJ Bell stadium.

Our relationship and standing with the RFL has never been stronger and this is due to the club being outward looking and showing how relevant we are to the game and leading on certain initiatives.

I would like to say thank you to my fellow Directors who have worked tirelessly to ensure the club has met the many challenges in the past year and we will be in a strong position to face the every changing landscape of our beloved game, however that may look in the new broadcasting deal commencing 2022.

I started by saying this is an exciting journey and this is a fantastic time to be part of the Lions family, and together we can enjoy this journey so let's all get behind the boys. This is a special time and I cannot wait until you are all allowed back at Heywood Road and creating our unique special atmosphere. In the meantime I encourage you to purchase the streaming packages as it assists the club and you don't miss the action.

I look forward to renewing acquaintance with you all.

Please keep safe.

Stuart Fletcher, Chairman, on behalf of The Board

LIONS DEFEAT NEWCASTLE IN CHALLENGE CUP ROUND ONE!
22 March 2021
The Lions booked their place in the next round of the Challenge Cup after a fantastic defensive display in the second half that thwarted a Thunder fightback led by former Wigan dual registration player Josh Woods.

Swinton Lions 28-16 Newcastle Thunder
The Lions suffered an early blow when Liam Forsyth had to leave the field with a leg injury and Rhodri Lloyd moved to the centres to take his place with Louis Brogan coming on to replace Forsyth. And in fact it was Lloyd

who opened the Lions try account in the eleventh minute when Martyn Ridyard set up an attack on the right and the Lions scored about ten metres from the corner with Ridyard adding the conversion points. Thunder tried to hit back eight minutes later when Evan Simons made a dart for the line but his try was cancelled out for a double movement.

Lions stretched their lead on the half hour mark when Mike Butt raced onto a Ridyard kick to score on the left and claim his three hundredth point in a Lions shirt and try creator Ridyard again made no mistake with the conversion. In the final minutes of the half Ridyard tried to add a drop goal but it dropped wide and from the restart on the twenty Thunder made good progress down the field and as the half time hooter sounded they forced the play and threw out a long pass to the right but the Lions were wise to it and Butt collected it about twenty metres out and raced away to score his second try of the evening, but the conversion attempt from Ridyard hit the posts and bounced out but the Lions held a sixteen point lead at the break.

Thunder started strong in the second half and Ted Chapelhow was held up over the line in the first couple of minutes. They continued their pressure on the Lions line and on forty-nine minutes it looked like Jack Johnson might score on the left but some great defence took him into touch. Ukuma Ta'ai opened the Thunder try account when he went over on the right after a good pass by Woods and Matty Wright added the conversion from close to the touchline. Ta'ai had a second try wiped off by the referee on sixty-one minutes for a knock on and the Lions defence was being made to work overtime to keep Thunder out.

Jack Hansen added the Lions next try two minutes later when Paul Nash, Lewis Hatton and Geronimo Doyle all combined to put the scrum half in under the posts and Ridyard converted again to put his side sixteen points ahead. Thunder then struck back with two tries in seven minutes masterminded by Woods with firstly Cian Tyrer going over on the right and this was converted and then Sam Wilde went over on the left but this time the conversion was missed but Thunder were now only six points behind with seven minutes remaining on the clock.

Captain Rhodri to the rescue as the Lions captain made a super break down the right with three minutes left and fed a nice pass for Doyle who got past the Thunder fullback to score under the posts and Ridyard made no mistake with the conversion meaning the Lions are in the next round.

Ian Rigg at Heywood Road

Tries: Lloyd (11), Butt (30,40), Hansen (63), Doyle (77)
Goals: Ridyard 4/5
Scoring Sequence: 6-0, 2-0, 16-0, 16-6, 22-6, 22-12, 22-16, 28-16.
Half-time: 16-0
Referee: Scott Mikalauskas

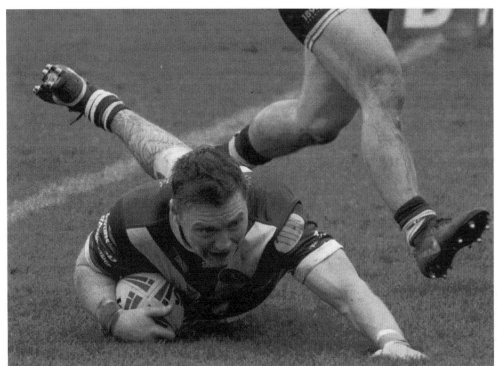

Above: Will Hope scores a try against Oldham in the Challenge Cup
Below: (Left) Will Hope, Luke Waterworth and Nick Gregson hold off an
Oldham attack Below (Right); Martyn Ridyard

SWINTON BEAT OLDHAM TO REACH CHALLENGE CUP ROUND 3 AND 1895 CUP SEMI-FINAL
29 March 2021

A strong second half performance by the Lions against a strong wind put them in the hat for the next round of the challenge cup and also earned them a semi-final place in the 1895 cup.

Swinton Lions 23-14 Oldham

It didn't start well for the Lions as Martyn Ridyard's kick off sailed straight dead to put Oldham on the attack straight away and they almost took the chance when Ryan Ince twice went close in the first five minutes but on both occasions the ball went loose. The Lions however came back strongly when Rhodri Lloyd broke free to feed the supporting Sam Grant

who raced away for the opening try and Ridyard added the conversion.

Oldham were throwing the ball around without fear against the conditions and almost got on the board when Max Roberts broke free to feed the pass to Ince but it was judged forward and Ben Heaton also broke down the middle but was stopped by a great tackle by Mike Butt ten metres out. Eventually they did break the Lions defence seventeen minutes from the break when the impressive Danny Langtree scored in the left corner but Dan Abram could not convert from the touchline.

The Lions made the ideal start to the second half when three minutes in a lovely short pass from Luke Waterworth sent Will Hope through a huge gap and he raced away to score by the posts with Ridyard adding the conversion. Oldham were not lying down and a couple of minutes later some great pressure on the line saw Tyler Dupree go over by the posts with Abram converting this one from close range.

Ridyard increased the Lions lead on fifty minutes when he darted over from close range to score by the posts and also add the conversion. A few minutes later they were in again when Ridyard and Jack Hansen combined to send

Deane Meadows racing twenty metres to score in the right corner but this time Ridyard could not convert off the touchline.

Matt Diskin would have been happy with his side as again they came back to pressure the Lions line and Martyn Reilly had a good chance but the Lions defence held true and then Shaun Pick looked like he was going over to score but the ball went free. Back came the Lions again but they blew a big chance just before the hour mark when former Oldham man Richard Lepori broke free and the inside pass to the supporting Hansen went to ground with the line open. On the next Lions set they made the game safe when Ridyard slotted over a drop goal.

It was Oldham who got the final points in the game with four minutes later when a good passing movement finished with Ben Heaton scoring in the right corner but again Abram could not add the conversion.

Ian Rigg at Heywood Road

LIONS
1 Mike Butt
2 Richard Lepori
3 Mitch Cox
5 Sam Grant
25 Luis Roberts
6 Martyn Ridyard
7 Jack Hansen
15 Luis Brogan
9 Luke Waterworth
10 Lewis Hatton
11 Rhodri Lloyd
12 Nick Gregson
13 Will Hope
Subs (all used)
24 Paul Nash
20 Tayler Brown
14 Billy Brickhill
19 Deane Meadows

Tries: Grant (5), Hope (43), Ridyard (50), Meadows (56)
Goals: Ridyard 3/4
Field Goal: Ridyard – 1
Scoring Sequence: 6-0, 6-4, 12-4, 12-10, 18-10, 22-10, 23-10, 23-14
Referee: Tom Grant

KEY & EAGLE
DIGITAL MEDIA

 Web Design

 Social Media

 Graphic Design

 Digital Marketing

 Search Engine
Optimisation

WWW.KEYANDEAGLE.COM

April

LIONS' LEGEND BOB FLEET STRENGTHENS TIES WITH DEVON SHARKS!

01 April 2021

In August 2020 we were thrilled to announce a community partnership arrangement with Devon Sharks ARLFC of the Southern Conference League. Despite covid restrictions the partnership has continued to strengthen, to the point where we can now proudly announce that

Swinton's very own most famous son of Devon, Bob Fleet, has agreed to become Honorary Patron of the Sharks.

Bob of course needs no introduction in Swinton or Devon rugby circles. Born at Torquay, he played for his county at Rugby Union before joining the Lions in 1960. He went on to become a star in the Swinton team that won back-to-back Championships in 1963 and 1964, before captaining the Lions to their 1969 Lancashire Cup triumph. He made a total of 376 appearances for Lions, scoring 90 tries. As a former Swinton player, coach, director, county representative and avid match day supporter, he certainly holds the most unique set of positions in the history of the club!

Stuart Fletcher, Chairman of Swinton Lions, said, "I am extremely pleased to confirm that Bob Fleet has agreed to become Honorary Patron of Devon Sharks. Bob needs no introduction to Lions' supporters having had such an illustrious career at the club, whilst his personal links to Devon will enable his vast knowledge to be utilised to assist the Sharks' progress in their inaugural season in the Southern Conference.

"This appointment reinforces the longstanding link between the Lions and Sharks which goes back to 2006 when Swinton donated their very first kit – the blue and white colours of which the Sharks have returned to for the 2021 season."

Bob pictured in Devon RU colours before signing for Swinton.

Phil Johnson, Director of Rugby at Devon Sharks, said, "We at the Sharks are very pleased to welcome Bob Fleet as Honorary Club Patron, alongside Andrew Henderson who we announced last year. Bob played for Torquay and Devon before signing for Swinton Lions and his vast knowledge will be of great assistance as we progress to become the most successful Rugby League Club in the South West. Welcome Bob to the Sharks family!"

Bob responded in typically modest fashion. He added, "I am greatly honoured to accept the invitation to become Honorary Patron of Devon Sharks ARLFC. Some 60 odd years ago I played my last games for Torquay Athletic and Devon RU before commencing on a wonderful career with Swinton Lions RLFC. Upon retiring from playing I then became President of the Lancashire County Rugby League…and it took a Devonian to do it!

"Indeed there is much pride in coming full circle and back to where it all began, especially in encompassing the exciting partnership between Devon Sharks and Swinton Lions. Long may it continue! Meanwhile, I look forward to being with you all in the not too distant future … sans boots! Best wishes, Bob Fleet."

LIONS LOSE CHAMPIONSHIP OPENER TO OLDHAM
03 April 2021

The 2021 Betfred Championship season got underway on Good Friday when the Lions again faced Oldham but fell to a disappointing loss after a poor second half.

Oldham 28-20 Swinton Lions

Oldham opened the scoring on five minutes when Dave Hewitt and Dan Abram combined to send Max Roberts over on the left and Abram converted. Ben Heaton was sent to the sin bin a few minutes later for obstruction and while he was cooling his heels the Lions opened their account when some good pressure saw Mike Butt score on the left but

Martyn Ridyard could not convert. Oldham stretched their lead when Dec Gregory and Hewitt combined again down the left and Ryan Ince went over for the try but Abram missed this conversion.

The scores were locked at ten each on twenty minutes when Luke Waterworth darted over by the posts and Ridyard converted this one and with thirteen minutes to go to the break, Ridyard kicked a forty-twenty and the Lions made them pay when Rhodri Lloyd finished off a move to score on the right but again this conversion was missed.

The Lions fourth try came on the half hour mark when Ridyard sent a low kick towards the posts and the ball came back off them and was collected by the chasing Jack Hansen but as he tried to control the ball he was hit by an illegal tackle and a penalty try was awarded. Ridyard then added the simple conversion to give them a ten point advantage at the break.

Oldham came out all cylinders firing in the second half and scored the first try after seven minutes when Ben Heaton went over but Abram could not convert and then Nick Gregson had the ball stolen one on one in a tackle and Tyler Dupree raced away forty metres to score in the right corner. Abram did convert this one to lock the scores at twenty all.

Lloyd looked as though he had scored for the Lions on fifty-four minutes but this was ruled out for a knock on and the chance went. Tom Spencer was sent off by referee Cameron Worsley on sixty-four minutes for an alleged punch in a tackle and the Lions were up against it with the hosts throwing everything at them. Heaton soon added his second try when Danny Langtree put him through a large gap and Abram converted to put them six points ahead. The final nail in the Lions coffin came with seven minutes left when Oldham were awarded a penalty just inside the Lions half and then someone said a word out of turn to the official and he marched them ten metres closer to the posts where Abram converted the simple penalty to secure the points for his side.

Ian Rigg at Bower Fold

LIONS KNOCKED OUT IN CHALLENGE CUP ROUND 3
12 April 2021

Warrington Wolves may be into the next round with a game against Catalans Dragons but my they will know they have been in a game because in a pulsating cup tie the Lions showed some great attacking flair and some real dogged defence and they were made to work hard for their victory.

Swinton Lions 8-32 Warrington Wolves

The game had some great build up during the week with the will he won't he make his debut story on Greg Inglis and the return of the Lions fans favourite Matty Ashton to the ground where he made his name in 2019. In the end it was Ashton who was named in the team to start at full back and

Inglis was forced to sit out another week waiting for full fitness and his debut.

The Lions made a really bright start in the early exchanges but it was Toby King who put the Wolves ahead in the sixth minute when they got a set restart and the ball was moved swiftly to the left where he strode over to score but Stefan Ratchford could not convert from the touchline. They nearly added a second a couple of minutes later down the left but the final pass went to ground.

Richard Lepori thought he had grabbed the opener for the Lions when he went over in the corner but there had been a knock on in the build-up and from the play the ball near their own line Wolves too lost the ball to put the Lions back on the attack. This time Swinton made them pay when a good passing movement allowed Luis Roberts to swallow dive in at the corner for the try and Martyn Ridyard converted from the touchline to put the Lions ahead.

It was now the Lions who were attacking the Wolves line and time after time they were breaking through down the right side and Jack Hansen went close eventually forcing a goal line drop out. This attack ended with a penalty for the Lions in front of the posts and Ridyard slotted over the simple kick to stretch the Lions lead.

Lepori had another great chance for the Lions with a break down the right forcing a good tackle by Ashton to stop him scoring and then another Wolves chance went away from them as the ball hit the ground again. The scores were level thirteen minutes from the break when King fed Tom Lineham to score in the left corner but Ratchford again missed the conversion.

King then added his second try five minutes later when he again went over on the left after the Lions had been penalised for a ball steal and this time Ratchford did add the conversion. Just before the half time hooter Blake

Austin dummied his way to the line to score and Ratchford again converted from a difficult angle to give his team a twelve point advantage at the break.

The Lions started the second half just as they did the first causing the Wolves defence plenty of headaches and it was Lepori again who made another long distance break to come close to scoring but the defence just got to him in time. Lineham then had a good chance for the Wolves but the ball was lost about ten metres out. Ridyard tried to engineer a second try for Roberts on the wing but the final pass just looped over his head with the line open.

It had to happen that Ashton would return to his old club and score and of course it did on sixty seven minutes when he was on the end of a pass to dive over in the left corner and Ratchford again added the conversion to finally give his side a bit of daylight. From the restart the Lions went short with the kick off and the ball bounced away from a Wolves player straight into the arms of Sam Brooks but he was tackled by the on rushing Ashton who received a head knock as he dived in and had to be helped off the field by two doctors but was ok after the match.

Wolves increased their lead with seven minutes left when Danny Walker jinked his way over to score under the posts and Ratchford added the simple conversion. It was another short kick off from the Lions after this try too and again they won the ball but the Wolves defence held out.

The Lions were pressing the line right to the final hooter and maybe deserved more points for their efforts in the game but credit to both sides for a really entertaining encounter.

Ian Rigg at Heywood Road

LIONS:
1 Mike Butt
2 Richard Lepori
3 Mitch Cox
11 Rhodri Lloyd
25 Luis Roberts
6 Martyn Ridyard
7 Jack Hansen
8 Sam Brooks
9 Luke Waterworth
15 Louis Brogan
19 Deane Meadows
12 Nick Gregson
13 Will Hope
Subs (all used)
20 Tayler Brown
16 Paddy Jones
18 Cobi Green (D)
26 Jordan Brown (D)

WOLVES
17 Matty Ashton
2 Tom Lineham
18 Jake Mamo
4 Toby King
5 Josh Charnley
6 Blake Austin
1 Stefan Ratchford
8 Chris Hill
9 Daryl Clark
13 Joe Philbin
11 Ben Currie
22 Ellis Robson
14 Jason Clark
Subs (all used)
19 Robbie Mulhern
21 Rob Butler
15 Matt Davis
16 Danny Walker

Swinton: Try: Roberts (14) **Goals:** Ridyard 2/2
Warrington: Tries: King (6,32), Lineham (27), Austin (37), Ashton (67),Walker (73) **Goals:** Ratchford 4/6

LEWIS HATTON – UPDATE
13 April 2021

Lewis has undergone a successful operation today to reattach a bicep following an injury sustained in the recent home cup tie against Oldham.

However, unfortunately it seems unlikely that we will see Lewis in action again for the Lions this season.

Everyone at the club is naturally bitterly disappointed, and no doubt all our supporters will join us in extending our best wishes to Lewis for a speedy recovery.

FEATHERSTONE TAKE THE SPOILS DESPITE LIONS' VALIANT SECOND HALF EFFORT
19 April 2021

Featherstone Rovers bounced back from their cup exit last weekend to claim victory over the Lions with some clinical finishing running in seven tries in a fast flowing encounter.

Swinton Lions 6-36 Featherstone Rovers

James Webster made changes to his starting team and the Lions were no match for them in the early stages. Rovers opened the scoring in the first five minutes when a good passing movement ended with Tom Holmes sending Gareth Gale over on the left but Fa'amanu Brown could not add the conversion from the touch line.

The ball was going through hands at a blistering pace at times and the second try was just as good when Holmes this time chipped through the Lions defence and bounced between two defenders straight into Holmes who regathered to score and this time Brown did convert to give his side a ten point lead.

The third try quickly followed when Gale broke down the left to draw the defence and send Thomas Minns away to touchdown in the left corner, however there was no conversion and the Lions looked a little shell shocked.

It could have got even worse for the Lions on twenty-four minutes when Connor Jones shot through a gap and headed for the try line only to be brought back for a forward pass in the build-up. The home side almost got on the scoreboard on the half hour mark when Mike Butt went close but was tackled into touch.

Rovers' fourth try came six minutes before the break when Gale was tackled just short and from the play the ball it was fizzed to the right where Brad Day was on hand to crash over and Brown converted this one. With the half time hooter coming up they added another when Brett Ferres broke through to feed the supporting John Davies who ducked under a couple of tackles to score by the posts.

The Lions started brighter in the second half and they had the first chance when a measured kick by Martyn Ridyard was chased by Luis Roberts but the ball just ran away from him as he tried to touch it down.

Ben Blackmore scored the next Rovers try on fifty-six minutes when Holmes and Minns combined to put him over on the left but the conversion was missed.

The Lions then turned great defence into attack midway through the half when firstly Gale was unable to take a pass to score and from the resulting restart Mike Butt broke down the left to draw Craig Hall before passing to the supporting Mitch Cox who raced in to score and Ridyard converted.

In the latter stages of the game both sets of defence were made to work hard to keep each other out with firstly Craig Kopczak being held up just short of the line and then former Lion Frankie Halton thwarted an attack when he managed to knock a pass down to stop a Lions try. However, it was Blackmore who added his second try in the dying seconds when the ball was chipped over the top and he won the race to score in the left corner and as Brown added the touchline conversion the hooter sounded for the end of a good encounter.

Ian Rigg at Heywood Road

Swinton CEO **Steve Wild** said, "I felt we came back into it very strongly in the second half, but Featherstone's first half performance was as good as anything I've seen at this level in a good while. They were both solid defensively and clinical in attack."

LIONS
22 Geronimo Doyle
1 Mike Butt
3 Mitch Cox
25 Luis Roberts
2 Richard Lepori
6 Martyn Ridyard
7 Jack Hansen
15 Louis Brogan
9 Luke Waterworth
8 Sam Brooks
11 Rhodri Lloyd
13 Will Hope
39 Tom Spencer
Subs (all used)
5 Sam Grant
18 Cobi Green
16 Paddy Jones
26 Jordan Brown
Try: Cox (64)
Goal: Ridyard 1/1

Featherstone Tries: Gale (5), Holmes (15), Minns (17), Day (34), Davies (37), Blackmore (56,79)
Goals: Brown 4/7

Pride Builder Funding Brings In New Player on Loan   22nd April
Once again this season, the Pride Builder fund have been able to help the club deliver a quality player to the squad in the form of former Newcastle and Ottawa Aces forward Sam Luckley, initially on a short term loan. Sam brings the total number of the fund's involvement in players to six and once again, proves that your generosity plays a significant part in the clubs fight to keep it where it belongs, back up in the top tier of the Championship.

LIONS AND SALE FC AGREE LEASE EXTENSION AT HEYWOOD ROAD
23 April 2021

Swinton Lions and Sale FC are delighted to announce that an agreement has been reached for the Lions to remain at Heywood Road until at least the end of the 2023 season.

The renewal of the lease extends the existing agreement by a further three years, by which time Swinton will have played out of Sale for a total of eight seasons.

On behalf of the Lions, CEO **Steve Wild**, said, "Swinton Rugby League Club wishes to thank everyone at Sale FC for their continued support and co-operation.

"Sale FC have become friends as well as stadium landlords, and over the next 3 years I'm sure we will develop the relationship even further in the pursuit of success for both of our historic organisations.

"We have recently worked together closely on Covid and Behind Closed Doors protocol and have spoken about the potential for future joint initiatives, and this spirit of co-operation will undoubtedly continue once crowds are allowed back in the ground.

"The facilities at Sale are absolutely superb, and are greatly appreciated by our players, staff and fans. Also, in being so close to the motorway and tram networks, it's a tremendously well-situated venue for all Greater Manchester rugby league and rugby union followers."

On behalf of Sale FC Rugby, **James Hourihan**, President, added, "Very much like Sale FC, Swinton Lions are a team with a proud history. Between our two great clubs we've been playing rugby for 330 years. This makes our relationship unique, not just in the world of rugby, but in sport as a whole.

"We are delighted that for the last five of those 155 years the Lions have chosen Heywood Road as their "home away from home" and we are thrilled that our new agreement extends this for at least another three years.

"We cannot wait for the stadium to be open and to be able to welcome the Lions' faithful back through the gates, to support the team they love, playing the greatest sport in the world – Rugby. Whether League or Union, we are united in our passion."

LIONESSES MAKE HISTORY!
24 April 2021

History was made this morning when the Swinton Lionesses Under 16s team took to the field for the very first time!

The game was played at Folly Lane's Blue Ribbon Field at Pendlebury, and was therefore effectively the first occasion that a team under the Swinton Lions banner had played in the M27 post code in some 29 years. In a strange twist of fate, Simon Ashcroft's daughter Eve featured for the Lionesses – Simon of course having made his Swinton debut in the Lions' first post-Station Road game back in 1992.

Sadly owing to Covid protocol currently governing community Rugby League, there was only extremely limited immediate family and club officials permitted to see the game, but hopefully before too long the Lionesses will be able to welcome a wider audience.

Facing the Lionesses was a strong and experienced Elland team from West Yorkshire, but the home team got off to a blistering start and raced into a 22-0 lead in the first half. Skye Johnson made history with the first try, whilst Ellie Thirkell scored a couple – one of which was particularly special. Ruth Boamah also scored a fine try, and full-back Maddison Higson added 3 conversions.

In a hotly contested second-half, Elland took advantage of their experience and the widening spaces as the Lionesses understandably tired in the warm sun. But although a late converted try snatched it for Elland, the final score was irrelevant on this memorable day in the history of Swinton Rugby League Club.

Every one of the Lionesses did themselves and their new team proud!

SWINTON LIONESSES U16s 22
ELLAND U16s 24

LIONESSES: Maddison Higson (3 goals); Eve Ashcroft; Catherine Sweeney;

Ruth Boamah (1 try); Mollie Scotson; Ellie Thirkell (2 tries); Skye Johnson (try); Abbie Parkes-Holden; Sophie Martins-Featherston; Emily Haley.

LIONS FALL TO A DISAPPOINTING DEFEAT DESPITE POSITIVE SECOND HALF EFFORT
26 April 2021
York City Knights got their first victory running in eleven tries against the Lions on their own patch with Matty Marsh scoring four of them.

Swinton Lions 16-64 York City Knights
Kieran Dixon who scored twenty-four points in the match scored the well

created opening try after three minutes and in fact the conversion attempt was the only one he missed in the whole game.

This was quickly followed by a Ronan Dixon try under the posts created by Marsh and the conversion was added. Marsh then scored a try of his own when he

wrong footed Geronimo Doyle to go under the posts with Dixon converting.

Ronan Dixon was leading from the front and he grabbed his second also scoring under the posts and taking two defenders with him and again the easy conversion was added. Marsh was making good things happen for the Knights and he broke through the Lions defence to feed the supporting loanee Connor Wynne who beat Doyle to score another converted try. There was a huge blow for the Lions when the playmaker Martyn Ridyard picked up a lower leg injury and had to hobble off the pitch never to return.

The Knights were playing some great attacking rugby in the sunshine and with ten minutes to go to the break, Danny Kirmond made a break down the right and drew in the Lions defence before handing the ball on to the supporting Marsh who raced away to claim his second with Dixon converting.

The Lions came out for the second half and made a very positive start when Jack Hansen unlocked the Knights defence to send the impressive Luis Roberts through a gap and he wrong footed Wynne to score by the posts and Hansen converted. The Knights hit back straight away with two more quick fire tries with Dean scoring the first after a good break and then Marsh completed his hat trick with Dixon converting both.

Will Hope was sent to the sin bin for a tip tackle on fifty-four minutes and from the penalty pressure Will Jubb sent a nice short kick to the Lions line and Ryan Atkins scored on the left. Just after the Atkins try the Lions were reduced to eleven men when Nick Gregson was sent to the sin bin for a shoulder on a Knights attacker and they scored again from the penalty when Dean went over by the posts.

The Lions had a good ten-minute spell in the final quarter and added two further tries when Mike Butt scored in the left corner and then Louis Brogan was sent through a gap by Hansen and he raced forty metres to score under the posts. Hansen converted this one but it was man of the moment Marsh who had the final word when he scored his fourth try in the dying seconds and Kieran Dixon added his tenth conversion of the afternoon.

Ian Rigg at Heywood Road
LIONS
22 Geronimo Doyle
1 Mike Butt
3 Mitch Cox
25 Luis Roberts
5 Sam Grant
6 Martyn Ridyard
7 Jack Hansen
8 Sam Brooks
9 Luke Waterworth
15 Louis Brogan
11 Rhodri Lloyd
12 Nick Gregson
13 Will Hope
Subs (all used)
39 Tom Spencer
16 Paddy Jones
38 Sam Luckley
24 Paul Nash

Tries: Roberts (41), Butt (70), Brogan (72)
Goals: Hansen 2/3

Congratulations to Luke Waterworth who made his 100th appearance for Swinton Lions against the York City Knights.

LIONS BRING IN SAINTS CENTRE ON LOAN
28 April 2021

At Swinton Lions we are pleased to report the signing of St Helens centre or winger Nico Rizzelli on an initial two-week loan deal.

Nico turned 21 last month and stands 5 feet 11 inches. He made his Super League debut last October against Salford and is highly rated by the Saints.

Currently he has tough opposition for the outside-back positions at the Totally Wicked Stadium, and therefore the player and both clubs involved see the loan has an ideal opportunity for Nico to get some valuable and competitive game time.

Swinton Lions would like to thank St Helens RLFC for their co-operation and support in agreeing the loan arrangements.

May
WIDNES VIKINGS 46-10 SWINTON LIONS
04 May 2021

The Lions travelled to Merseyside to take on the Vikings who have also been struggling to find any form this season.

Swinton made a very bright start with continuous pressure on the Vikings line for almost the first half hour of the match but they could not find any cutting edge to break the defence.

Sam Luckley came the closest when he got over the try line but could not hold the pass and the Vikings got to the restart quickly on the twenty to move down field and open the scoring very much against the run of play when Deon Cross finished off a move to go over in the corner. Steve Tyrer converted from the touchline.

Six minutes later they were in for a second when Matty Smith chip kicked a ball to the left and Kenny Baker was on hand to take the catch and touchdown with Tyrer again converting. With three minutes to go to the break, hooker Brad O'Neill went through a huge gap in the Lions defence to score by the posts again converted by Tyrer.

The Lions half time team talk didn't work as Jack Owens found Tyrer and he scored out wide but he was unable to convert his own try and this was followed by a try by Warrington loanee Ellis Robson who scored under the posts and this was again converted.

The Lions got on the scoreboard after fifty-three minutes when Luis Roberts fired out a pass for Nico Rizzelli to dive over in the right corner but Jack Hansen could not add the extras from the touchline. However, it was the Vikings who took control again punching huge holes in the Lions defence with Shane Gray, Adam Lawton and Cross all going over for tries and Tyrer converted all three of them. It was the Lions who scored the final try of the game with Mike Butt going over for his fourth try in four games at the DCBL Stadium and Hansen added the conversion to complete the scoring.

Ian Rigg at the DCBL Stadium
Lions: Doyle, Butt, Cox, Roberts, Rizzelli, Gregson, Hansen, Brogan, Nash, Luckley, Lloyd, Meadows, Hope. Subs: Brickhill, Brooks, Spencer, Green.
Referee: Jack Smith

JACOB SMILLIE LEAVES LIONS
05 May 2021
Swinton Lions RLFC can announce that by mutual consent it has parted company with winger Jacob Smillie.

Sadly since joining the Lions from Bradford Bulls last October, Jacob has developed an ongoing injury which has hampered his development and progress. Jacob himself has stated that he has chosen to pursue a different path outside of Rugby

League, and the club has therefore agreed to his request to release him from his contract.

Jacob leaves us on friendly terms a

LIONS CELEBRATE 125th ANNIVERSARY.
07 May 2021
Lions mark 125 years of Rugby League!

On this day exactly 125 years ago (7th May 1896), and having resigned from the Rugby Football Union, the Swinton club was formally admitted to what was then the Northern Rugby Union (which now of course is called the Rugby Football League).

The last 125 years have witnessed the highest of highs and the lowest of lows, but still the Lions battle on as one of the most famous names in the sport!

At Swinton we are rightly extremely proud of our heritage, and to mark this special anniversary we will shortly be revealing something rather special – so keep an eye on our social media channels over the next few days!

BULLS EDGE LIONS IN THRILLER AT HEYWOOD ROAD
10 May 2021

A great second half fightback by the Lions almost snatched the points from the Bulls in the last ten minutes and a Jordan Lilley drop goal midway through the half proved the winner in the end.

Swinton Lions 22-23 Bradford Bulls

The Lions started brightly and opened the scoring in the seventh minute

when on loan Saints player Nico Rizzelli crashed over in the corner after some smart play by Geronimo Doyle but Martyn Ridyard was unable to add the conversion. Bulls tried to hit back and there was some good play by both Danny Brough and Lilley but ball handling errors in finishing off the good work let them down.

David Foggin-Johnston looked like he might score in the corner but the ball came loose as he went for the line, however in the next Bulls set hooker Thomas Doyle found a gap to score under the posts and Brough converted.

Deane Meadows should really have put the Lions back in the lead but his kick for the line was too strong and rolled dead. From the twenty metre restart Bulls went down field and Foggin-Johnston this time supported Brandon Pickersgill's break to score in the left corner and Brough slotted the conversion from the touchline.

There was then another chance for the Bulls winger but the kick was too strong and Mike Butt also had a chance created by Jack Hansen but again too much speed on the kick.

It was Pickersgill who again created the next try when he broke free to feed Brough and he scored under the posts and converted his own try. The Lions were not lying down and with twenty seconds to go to the break Luis Roberts broke several tackles to score under the posts as the hooter sounded and Ridyard converted to put the Lions eight behind at Half-Time.

It was a scrappy start to the second half with the Lions knocking on at the kick-off and lots of lost ball from both sides, but it was the Bulls who scored first when Pickersgill got a deserved try but Brough failed to convert. Luis Roberts had to leave the field after a late hit on fifty-two minutes and never returned so the Lions had to regroup.

Then they lost Luke Waterworth who was sent to the sin bin for holding down and while he was off, Lilley added a drop goal to stretch the advantage. The Lions then had two good chances through Butt and Rhodri Lloyd and they added their fourth try when Rizzelli put in a nice reverse pass for Lloyd to go over in the corner and reduce the angle for Ridyards conversion.

Three minutes later they were in again when Lloyd this time made the break and fed the supporting Hansen who raced under the posts and again Ridyard converted to set up a grandstand finish. In the final few minutes the Bulls had another chance to score but Rizzelli was on hand to stop the attack by knocking the ball dead.

Ian Rigg at Heywood Road
LIONS
Tries: Riizzelli (7), Roberts (40), Lloyd (68), Hansen (71)
Goals: ¾
Sin-Bin: Waterworth (58) Holding Down

BULLS
Tries: Doyle (19), Foggin-Johnston (26), Brough (35), Pickersgill (49)
Goals: Brough ¾
Field Goal: Lilley – 1

LIONS CELEBRATE 125 YEAR OF RUGBY LEAGUE WITH SUPERB ANNIVERSARY KIT!

17 May 2021

This month at Swinton Lions we celebrate the club's 125th year of playing Rugby League Football.

Back in May 1896, having resigned from the Rugby Football Union, Swinton successfully applied to join the fledgling Northern Union, which had been formed just a few months earlier. This of course is what we now know as the Rugby Football League.

Just four seasons later, under the leadership of the legendary Jim Valentine, the Lions won the Challenge Cup, thus beginning the series of highs and lows which now form our magnificent history and heritage.

To mark this 125th Anniversary, in collaboration with our team wear partners SUPRO, we have commissioned a magnificent playing kit. This kit will be worn only once – in our match against Dewsbury Rams – but our fans will have the opportunity to own a limited-edition replica.

The all navy blue design is a nod to our original colours, as is the decision to strip back commercial logos with the kind consent of our club sponsors. The lion in shadow and other design features then give it a modern twist which we hope will prove a hit with fans of all ages.

Just 125 shirts will be available on a first come first basis – so please purchase early to avoid disappointment. Note that each of the 125 shirts will be individually tagged with its own unique number.

RAMS WIN DESPITE LATE SECOND HALF FIGHTBACK
18 May 2021
Monday night saw the return of fans to Heywood Road but a strong first half from the visitors saw them take home the points despite a late Lions rally.

Swinton Lions 18-20 Dewsbury Rams

Rams took the lead in the third minute when a good passing movement saw Andy Gabriel crash over in the right corner but Paul Sykes was unable to

convert. The Lions then had two good chances with Luis Roberts making a nice break down the right but ran out of support and then Jack Hansen kicked the ball through the Rams defence

towards the line but the ball ran away from him.

Rams then went further ahead when they got a six again and Michael Knowles went over on the left and again Sykes was off target with the kick. On twenty minutes Keenen Tomlinson latched onto a Sykes kick to score by the posts and this time Sykes converted to give them a good advantage on the scoreboard.

Mike Butt then had a great chance when Martyn Ridyard put a kick in down the left but the flying winger was offside when he collected the ball. Paddy Jones was sent to the sin bin eleven minutes from the break for an illegal tackle on Aaron Hall and Sykes kicked the penalty to give them a good lead at the break.

The Lions started the fightback on fifty-one minutes when Mitch Cox went through several tacklers to score on the left with Ridyard converting from the touchline and a few minutes later Louis Brogan thought he had scored but was just held up over the line.

Sykes then increased the Rams lead with two simple penalties in a six minute period. The Lions then hit a purple patch in the last six minutes of the game when Billy Brickhill broke through to score by the posts and Ridyard converted.

With four minutes to go he repeated the same move to score by the posts and Ridyard again converted but time ran out.

Ian Rigg at Heywood Road
Swinton – Doyle, Roberts, Rizzelli, Cox, Butt, Ridyard, Hansen, Brooks, Waterworth, Luckley, Lloyd, Meadows, Hope. **Subs:** Birckhill, Brogan, Jones, Spencer.

Loanees Recalled
20th May 2021

We can confirm that Nico Rizzelli and Sam Luckley have both been recalled by their parent clubs following loan stints with the Lions. Both Nico and Sam have said that they've enjoyed their time at the club, despite of course recent results. We'd like to thank both lads for their efforts on behalf of Swinton Lions.

REBECCA TO CAPTAIN THE LIONESSES!
21 May 2021

Ahead of the Swinton Lionesses open-age team's debut this coming weekend, Head Coach Martina Greenwood has selected her first team captain.

Rebecca Roden will already be well known to many Swinton fans, as of course she is an avid supporter of the Lions herself. It therefore seems very appropriate to have a Swintonian installed as the women's first skipper.

Martina explained, "I am very pleased to announce that our first ever woman to captain a Swinton Lionesses team is Rebecca Roden. I rang Rebecca and her family on Thursday evening to let her know and she was delighted and honoured to have been chosen. The players are now looking forward to their first ever women's clash against a formidable Fryston team on Sunday."
Rebecca has also received many congratulatory messages from her team-mates, to which she replied, "I am so honoured to be named the captain of our team! We have a great bunch of girls and I cannot wait to be playing alongside you all! Let's go girls 2021!"

Swinton Lions Pride Builder
Sort Code: 30-92-92
Account No: 37544168

Having hosted Two Toulouse games at Heywood Road and as a thank you of appreciation of our hard work in arranging both games Stephen Wild and Stuart Fletcher were honoured to receive a signed Toulouse shirt from Cedric, CEO of Toulouse Olympique. The friendship between the two club's continue to blossom.

TOULOUSE 66-18 SWINTON
23 May 2021

Toulouse continued their impressive run of high scoring victories running in twelve tries against the Lions who at one stage actually held the lead for a five minute period.

Because of Covid travel restrictions the game had to be switched to Heywood

Road but the small crowd were treated to some fast flowing rugby. Remi Casty put the home side into the lead in the third minute when he latched onto a Dominique Peyroux pass to score to the left of the posts and Mark Kheirallah added the conversion, which was quickly followed three minutes later when Junior Vaivai set up Anthony Marion for the second try but this time the conversion was unsuccessful. It looked ominous for the Lions but this was not to be and on their first attack Mitch Cox almost scored but managed to force a goal line drop out. From this they pressured the line and Martyn Ridyard set up the pass for the supporting Nick Gregson who broke through several tackles to score to the left of the posts and Ridyard added the simple conversion.

The second Lions try was well engineered with Gregson breaking a tackle in his own half to feed the supporting Geronimo Doyle who drew Kheirallah and then offloaded to Jack Hansen who raced thirty metres to score under the posts and Ridyard converted to put his side in the lead. Mattieu Jussaume then put Toulouse back in the lead on eighteen minutes and this was quickly followed by the first of the afternoon by Latrell Shaumkel but neither were converted keeping their six point advantage.

The Lions were not going away and they scored their third on twenty-five minutes when Ridyard kicked towards the posts and Johnathon Ford collected the ball and tried to play off his line, he then threw a pass meant for Vaivai but did not see Cox coming the other way and he took the pass to score by the posts and Ridyard converted to level the scores. However, Toulouse went into the break with the lead after a superb pass by the impressive Tony Gigot found Joe Bretherton and he scored by the posts with Kheirallah adding the conversion before the hooter.

Match Championship

TO XIII

contre

SWINTON LIONS

■

STADE HEYWOOD ROAD
Samedi 22 Mai 2021

PROGRAMME-SOUVENIR
£3.00 / €3.50

The home side went further ahead just after the restart when Gigot was the provider for a Mitch Garbutt try again converted. Rhodri Lloyd was sent to the sin bin on fifty two minutes for holding down and just after this an incident was put on report for something that happened in a tackle on Joe Bretherton and from the resulting penalty near the line came another try with Eloi Pelissier going over and this was again converted.

This was quickly followed by a converted try by Kheirallah set up by Ford. Gregson almost added a second for the Lions on the hour but some good tackling held him out.

Toulouse passed the fifty point mark when Schaumkel grabbed a brace in a six minute period to complete his hat trick and both were converted. Another good chance for the Lions with five minutes left when Luis Roberts and Hansen combined but the ball went to ground near the line but Toulouse finished strong with two further tries in the last three minutes with Peyroux and Ford both going in for well worked efforts and again both were converted to complete the victory.
Ian Rigg at Heywood Road

TOULOUSE

1 Mark Kheirallah
2 Jy Hitchcox
4 Mattieu Jussaume
3 Junior Vaivai
21 Latrell Schaumkel
6 Johnathon Ford
31 Tony Gigot
8 Remi Casty
9 Lloyd White
10 Harrison Hansen
16 Joe Bretherton
12 Dominique Peyroux
13 Anthony Marion
Subs (all used)
14 Eloi Pelissier
18 Mitch Garbutt
23 Justin Sangare
27 Maxine Garcia

Tries: Casty (3), Marion (6), Jussaume (18), Schaumkel (20,63,69), Bretherton (39), Garbutt (46), Pelissier (53), Kheirallah (56), Peyroux (77), Ford (78).   **Goals**: Kheirallah 9/12

LIONS

22 Geronimo Doyle
1 Mike Butt
3 Mitch Cox
11 Rhodri Lloyd
25 Luis Roberts
6 Martyn Ridyard
7 Jack Hansen
8 Sam Brooks
9 Luke Waterworth
26 Jordan Brown
19 Deane Meadows
12 Nick Gregson
14 Billy Brickhill
Subs (all used)
16 Paddy Jones
21 Ben Heyes
24 Paul Nash
20 Tayler Brown

Tries: Gregson (11), Hansen (13), Cox (25) **Goals**: Ridyard 3/3

Above: The tries scored against Toulouse.

GIANT RONAN JOINS THE LIONS
27 May 2021

We are pleased to announce the loan signing of Irish International prop-forward Ronan Michael from Huddersfield Giants.

Ronan emerged through the Lions' community partner club, Dublin Longhorns, and made his Super League debut for the Giants late in 2020.

20 years old Ronan has recently been on loan with Whitehaven, but has jumped at the chance to join Swinton.

HAMLETT JOINS LIONS ON LOAN
28 May 2021

Swinton Lions RLFC wishes to announce the loan signing of powerful 6 foot Bradford Bulls three-quarter Reece Hamlett.

Warrington Wolves brought Reece in last year from Wigan as part of their reserve and fringe first team set up, but when the reserve league was mothballed owing to covid he jumped at the chance to join the Bulls.

A former England Youth International, Reece had an impressive game for Bradford in the recent pre-season friendly against the Lions, and will add size and strength to the Swinton back line.

BATLEY BULLDOGS 26-12 SWINTON LIONS

31 May 2021

The Bulldogs got back to winning ways with a strong second half performance down the slope that took the game away from the Lions after such a good performance in the first half.

The Lions made a great start with a short kick off which put them straight on the attack, and within fifty seconds Mitch Cox found a gap in the Bulldogs defence to go through to score his third try in three matches but Martyn Ridyard could not convert from the touchline.

It could have been better for the Lions on seven minutes when Jack Hansen broke clear but his final pass to Luis Roberts fell behind him and into touch. Bulldogs then had two good chances with Jodie Broughton going for the left corner and being tackled into touch and then Adam Gledhill got over the line but was grounded on his back.

Luke Hooley should really have scored on twelve minutes when former Lion Ben White sent him through a gap by the line but he could not hold the pass and the ball ran dead.

The Lions went further ahead a minute later when Nick Gregson broke through to send a reverse pass to Sam Brooks who touched down for his first try for the club and Ridyard added the simple conversion. The Lions were looking strong attacking the Bulldogs line but it was the home side who scored next when Alistair Leek went close and from the play the ball Ben Kaye dived over for the try and Dale Morton converted. And as the half time hooter sounded Ridyard tried to add a drop goal but that sailed wide.

Bulldogs made the best start to the second half when the Lions lost the ball in their own ten metres, and it finished with James Brown scoring under the posts with Morton adding the conversion. Despite the conditions there were lots of ball handling errors and the Bulldogs were continuing to pressure the line, however it was the Lions who drew level on the hour when they received two penalties in a row and on the second one Ridyard stroked over a nice thirty metre penalty goal from near the touchline. Five minutes later

Morton put the Bulldogs in the lead from in front of the posts when Luke Waterworth was sent to the sin bin for an off the ball tackle on Tom Gilmore.

Bulldogs then took control of the game in the final eight minutes when they introduced Elliot Hall at fullback and he created a try in the corner for Broughton and Morton converted off the touchline. With two minutes left Alistair Leek found a nice gap to score by the posts and Morton again converted to cement the victory.

Ian Rigg at The Fox's Biscuits Stadium

Batley
Tries: Kaye (24), Brown (41), Broughton (72), Leak (78)
Goals: Morton 5/5
LIONS
22 Geronimo Doyle
1 Mike Butt
3 Mitch Cox
39 Reece Hamlett
25 Luis Roberts
6 Martyn Ridyard
7 Jack Hansen
8 Sam Brooks
9 Luke Waterworth
40 Ronan Michael
11 Rhodri Lloyd
12 Nick Gregson
14 Billy Brickhill
Subs (all used)
16 Paddy Jones
20 Tayler Brown
19 Deane Meadows
18 Cobi Green
Tries: Cox(1), Brooks (13)
Goals: Ridyard 2/3

June

YORK CITY KNIGHTS 36-22 SWINTON LIONS
07 June 2021

The Lions gave their all to get the club to Wembley for the first time in their history but came up just short in a pulsating cup tie played in York's very impressive new stadium.

The Lions made a great start and had their first chance in the third minute when Mitch Cox almost got over in the left corner but a bounce of the ball went away from him. However, it was the Knights who took the lead two minutes later when Matty Marsh cut through the defence to send Liam Salter over for the try on the right and Kieran Dixon added the conversion.

Geronimo Doyle then had a great chance after a break by Mike Butt but was tackled just short of the line on the sixth tackle. Martyn Ridyard sent a kick towards the Knights line on twelve minutes and with Butt chasing the kick Marsh had no option but to boot it dead and the goal line drop out was awarded. From this the Lions put even more pressure on the Knights defence and a good passing movement down the left side saw Mike Butt open the scoring in the left corner and Ridyard added a super conversion from the touchline.

It got even better for the Lions five minutes later when from a six again Sam Brooks went close and from the play the ball Ronan Michael forced his way over by the posts for his first Swinton try with Ridyard added his second conversion to put the Lions into a deserved lead. But the Knights hit back after twenty-four minutes after a Lions goal line drop out substitute Marcus Stock went through several tackle attempts to score on the left and Dixon converted to lock the scores.

Luke Waterworth and Luis Roberts both had chances before again the Knights forced a second goal line drop out and again they scored from it when Marsh cut inside this time from the left to send veteran centre Ryan Atkins over and Dixon was again on target to give them a six point interval lead.

Kris Brining extended the Knights lead within two minutes of the restart when he scored by the posts and again this was converted by Dixon but the Lions tried to bounce back and Mitch Cox almost set up a try for Doyle but the final pass was forward. Again it was the Knights who went further ahead when Danny Kirmond scored on the right and this was converted but the Lions came back again when Rhodri Lloyd broke down the right to feed Roberts who sent a nice inside pass for Mike Butt to score his second, this time Ridyard's conversion attempt hit the posts and bounced out.

There was a bit of controversy on sixty-eight minutes when Nick Gregson was the victim of what looked like a crusher tackle and as he went down he lost the ball which the officials ruled a knock on. Despite the protests from the Lions players on the pitch and the coaching staff, in the end the incident was placed on report by referee Tom Grant but the play the ball still went to the Knights.

The Killer try came with eleven minutes left when the Lions were on the attack down the right and the ball went to ground on the Knights twenty and Mikey Lewis, the Hull KR player on loan, swooped up the ball to race eight metres to score under the posts with Dixon again making no mistake with the conversion.

The Lions did not give up all afternoon roared on by their noisy band of fans and the game finished with a hat trick try for Mike Butt in the dying minutes after Germonimo Doyle set it up for him and Ridyard added another great conversion from the touchline. A great game and a very proud effort from the Lions.

Ian Rigg at the LNER Community Stadium
LIONS

Doyle, Butt, Cox, Lloyd, Roberts, Ridyard, Hansen, Michael, Waterworth, Brooks, Meadows, Gregson, Brickhill. Subs: Jones, Brogan, Hope, Green.

Board Room Announcement
8 June 2021
The Board of Directors wishes to make the following statement.
During today's Board meeting, it very quickly became clear that our Head Coach Stuart Littler has the 100% unequivocal support of the entire Swinton Lions Board of Directors.

Whilst we are all naturally disappointed with our current league position, it is our firm belief that the club's interests are best served by demonstrating strength through unity. We therefore felt it important to make our position clear via this statement, as a firm response to any semblance of damaging speculation.

Alongside Stuart we have an outstanding coaching and back-room team, in whom the Board also has complete faith. We also have trust in our players to do everything within their own powers to secure the valuable wins that we need.

Stuart and our coaching staff team have never once cited injuries as the reason for our league position, but the fact remains that the strength of our squad has been severely affected by long-term and short-term injuries to key players. The Board is fully aware that we are currently short on playing numbers and will continue to support Stuart in identifying suitable additions to the squad.

Our fans were absolutely fantastic in their support of the team at York last Sunday, and this was greatly appreciated by the players and staff. With similar backing between now and the end of the season, we will stand the best chance of achieving our immediate goals.
Thank you for your support.
THE BOARD OF SWINTON LIONS RLFC

SWINTON SIGN BATLEY FORWARD ON LOAN
10 June 2021
The Lions can confirm the loan signing of Batley Bulldogs forward, Dominic Horn.

Dominic, who joined Batley in 2020, has been signed in time to come into consideration for Sunday's squad for the game against Newcastle Thunder at Heywood Road, kick-off 3pm.

The period of loan has initially been left open-ended, subject to how the loan progresses for Swinton, Batley and the player.

Welcome to Swinton Lions Dominic!

SWINTON LIONS 30-36 NEWCASTLE THUNDER

14 June 2021

Newcastle Thunder went home with the points having scored unopposed points in the first thirty minutes of the game but the Lions staged a fantastic fightback that almost took the points away from the visitors.

Ukuma Ta'ai opened the scoring on nine minutes and this was quickly followed by a short range effort from Bob Beswick and these were both converted by Josh Woods.

Thunder were on a roll with the Lions finding it hard to get the ball and it was the visitors who then ran in three quick tries with Matt Wright, Connor Bailey and Calum Turner going over and Woods added all three conversions. However, the Lions started the comeback on thirty-two minutes when Will Hope went over from short range and this was quickly followed when Mike Butt and Ben Heyes combined to send Mitch Cox over on the left and Ridyard converted both.

Try of the match contender came three minutes from the break when Thunder were on the attack and Ta'ai offloaded the ball straight into the arms of Nick Gregson and he raced nearly eighty metres to score under the posts and this again was converted.

Thunder went further ahead five minutes into the second half when Wright added his second but the conversion from Woods was missed. The second contender for try of the match came soon after when Sam Brooks came steaming onto a short pass to break away towards the Thunder full back and then passed the ball to Jack Hansen who raced in under the posts to claim his two hundredth point for the Lions, Ridyard converted again to put the Lions back in it.

Waterworth and Jay Chapelhow were then sent to the sin-bin for fighting. More pressure on the Thunder line on fifty-six minutes saw Will Hope go over for his second of the afternoon and this again was converted by Ridyard. They game was stopped on fifty-nine minutes for a serious medical incident and all the medics and doctors from both clubs were involved is stabilising the patient and getting them to hospital.

There was a break of about 30 minutes but the officials allowed the game to resume and play out the last twenty-one minutes and just after the restart Thunder were awarded a penalty for holding down and Wright added the kick to stretch the lead. The Lions tried as hard as they could but couldn't get past the Thunder defence in the final minutes and they held out to take the victory.

Ian Rigg at Heywood Road
LIONS
21 Ben Heyes
1 Mike Butt
3 Mitch Cox
11 Rhodri Lloyd
25 Luis Roberts
6 Martyn Ridyard
7 Jack Hansen
8 Sam Brooks
9 Luke Waterworth
13 Will Hope
19 Deane Meadows
12 Nick Gregson
13 Billy Brickhill
Subs (all used)
16 Paddy Jones
15 Louis Brogan
39 Dom Horn
24 Paul Nash (NU)
Tries: Hope (32,56), Cox (34),Gregson (37), Hansen (49)
Goals: Ridyard 5/5

Dave Jones

Many of you may know that the club President David Jones suffered a heart attack at the game today.

David was taken to Wythenshawe hospital where he was admitted to the resuscitation ICU.

Happily I can report that David is stable but very confused about the events leading up to his hospitalisation.

It's possible he will undergo an operation in the next few days to fit a defibrillation device according to his wife Pat.

She has told me that the hospital were full of praise for the actions of the medical team at the ground without which the outcome may have been fatal. Wishing David a speedy recovery.

Alan Marshall

The Club followed up Alan's message with an official comment:

After contact with David's family today, we can confirm that he is currently in a stable and more comfortable condition in hospital and receiving the best possible treatment. Once again, we would like to acknowledge and thank the magnificent efforts of our medical and support staff, who did an incredible job yesterday afternoon when assisting David. We would also like to thank Newcastle Thunder for their assistance and ongoing concern, as well all the Rugby League supporters from both inside and outside the Swinton Lions Family for their messages of goodwill. As and when we are able to pass on any further information we will do so. Thank you everyone.

RICHARD LEPORI
16 June 2021
Unfortunately, we have to confirm that following further medical advice, our winger Richard Lepori is likely to be out of action for several more weeks. This follows

a freak but unavoidable muscle accident in the club gym.

Richard is currently undergoing a detailed rehab programme under the guidance of the club's medical staff, and whilst there's no guarantee, it's hoped that he will be back in action for the Lions at the end of the season. Prior to the injury Richard's performances for Swinton had been first class, and we're sure that all Lions' fans will join us in wishing him a speedy recovery.

Tom Spencer
18th June 2021
We have re-initiated the loan agreement with Leigh Centurions for Tom Spencer. Tom rejoins us on an initial 2 week loan deal, with options to renew should things progress well for the player and both clubs. Swinton Lions would like to thank all at Leigh Centurions for their assistance in completing the necessary arrangements.

SWINTON LIONS 4-34 HALIFAX PANTHERS
21 June 2021
Halifax Panthers continued their good run with a six try victory over the Lions who again put in a good performance but were held out many times by the rock steady Panthers defence.

Panthers made a strong start but blew early chances losing the ball in good positions but eventually took the lead on seventeen minutes when Gadwin Springer and Ben

Kavanagh combined to send Scott Grix over under the posts and Liam Harris converted.

The Lions tried to hit back when Jack Hansen created a chance for Luis Roberts but the kick was well dealt with by James Woodburn-Hall. Roberts did get over the line a few minutes later but the final pass was forward and from this Panthers went down field and Grix added a second after some good attacking build up with Harris adding the conversion.

Grix almost scored his third on thirty-two minutes but was obstructed on the way to the line and from the penalty the ball moved swiftly across the line and Conor McGrath dived over by the corner flag but Harris hit the posts with his conversion attempt. Grix got over the line four minutes from the break but he was held up by Will Hope and from the play the ball again the ball was moved quickly to the right and McGrath went over for his second. Harris converted this one and they went into half-time with a good lead. The Lions made a good start to the second half and Roberts, Rhodri Lloyd and Mitch Cox all had good chances but again the defence from Panthers held them out. McGrath had another good chance to score but he was knocked into touch from a great tackle by debutant Dan Clare but the pressure paid off eventually when Kavanagh was sent through a large gap by Harris to score on the left and the try provider added the conversion. The Lions' determination eventually paid off on fifty-six minutes when a good passing movement ended with Luis Roberts diving in at the corner but Ridyard could not convert from the touchline. An incident was put on report just after the hour mark when Nick Rawsthorne seemed to be the victim of a crusher tackle and from the penalty, play moved down field and Amir Bourouh raced away to beat the Lions defence and score by the posts and Harris added the simple conversion.

Swinton prop forward Tom Spencer was sent to the sin bin five minutes from time for an obstruction and again from the penalty Panthers thought they had scored but Springer was pulled back for a forward pass. Both sides again had chances in the dying minutes of the game but neither could score and the large following of Panthers fans went home happy.

Ian Rigg at Heywood Road

LIONS
1 Mike Butt
28 Dan Clare (D)
3 Mitch Cox
11 Rhodri Lloyd
25 Luis Roberts
6 Martyn Ridyard
7 Jack Hansen
8 Sam Brooks
9 Luke Waterworth
39 Tom Spencer
13 Will Hope
12 Nick Gregson
14 Billy Brickhill
Subs (all used)
15 Louis Brogan
26 Jordan Brown
16 Paddy Jones
19 Deane Meadows
Try: Roberts (56)

Club Honours Heroes
21 June 2021
The Newcastle match was emotional for most who attended and after last week's traumatic event with our club president. At the Halifax match it was honour for Steve Wild and Stuart Fletcher to present life memberships to two unbelievable people who did get involved in a life and death scenario.

Katie Richardson and Paul Leadbetter were presented with their Club President's certificates for their efforts the previous week.

Above: Katie Richardson receives her Club President Certificate
Below: Paul Leadbetter receives his Club President Certificate

MATCH REPORT – LONDON BRONCOS 38-24 SWINTON LIONS

29 June 2021

The Lions played some of their best Rugby of the season in this game and were unlucky not to come away with something for their performance.

Rhodri Lloyd put the Lions

ahead after five minutes when Tom Spencer was grounded just short of the line by Chris Hankinson and from the play the ball Cobi Green sent a nice short pass for the Lions captain to go over on the right and Martyn Ridyard converted from near the touchline.

Broncos hit back on thirteen minutes when Gideon Boafo evaded tackles to score on the left and Hankinson converted, the same player was over for his second four minutes later when he scored in the left corner and Hankinson again added the goal points.

A Broncos player was placed on report for an illegal tackle on Mike Butt when he seemed to get knees in the back after collecting a high ball near his line and struggled with the injury until half time when he was substituted.

Broncos went further ahead on the half hour when Abbas Miski went over and Hankinson again converted but the Lions were not taking a back seat. Four minutes later Broncos were on the attack down their left just inside their own half and the ball went to ground and Green was following play, he scooped up the ball to race away and score his first Lions try with Ridyard again converting.

The Lions attack was frustrating the Broncos defence and just before the break Ridyard sent a kick towards the line and the Broncos winger Josh Hodson committed the sin of letting the ball bounce and it bounced away from him straight into the hands of the chasing Mitch Cox, who fed the supporting Mike Butt who scored in the left corner and Ridyard converted to level the scores at the break.

The injured Mike Butt did not return at half time and they had to reshuffle with Deane Meadows moving to the wing. Deane was the spark for the next try when he was grounded just short of the line and from the play the ball play moved swiftly right and Luis Roberts managed to squeeze over in the corner and Ridyard again converted from the touchline to put the Lions in a strong position. Broncos came back strongly with two tries in three minutes midway through the half with Boafo and Miski going over and Hankinson converted one of them to give them a four-point advantage.

Another incident was placed on report by referee Mike Smaill which saw Rhodri Lloyd victim of what looked like a crusher tackle. Luis Roberts left the field with a foot injury just after that incident and the Lions had to reshuffle the team again but it was Broncos who took the advantage in the final ten minutes with Will Lovell and Jarrod Sammut both going over for late tries and Hankinson

added one further conversion. The Lions never stopped battling and Nick Gregson made a very dangerous break in the last minutes but he was grounded just short.

Ian Rigg at Ealing Trailfinders
Lions
Hansen, Roberts, Lloyd, Cox, Butt, Ridyard, Green, Brooks, Waterworth, Spencer, Hope, Gregson, Brickhill. Subs: T.Brown, Jones, Meadows, Nash.

July

Mason Joins on Trial
04 July 2021
Cardiff born James Mason, a forward, joins us on a month's trial and goes straight into the Lions' squad to face Whitehaven this weekend. Welcome James!

MATCH REPORT –
WHITEHAVEN 36-22 SWINTON LIONS

06 July 2021
For the second time in two weeks the Lions got off to an excellent start only to fall short in the second half for the home side to take the points.

The game was only seven minutes old when Tom Spencer was grounded just short in front of the posts and from the play the ball Luke Waterworth fed Deane Meadows and he crashed over by the posts and Martyn Ridyard converted.

Rhodri Lloyd and Lachlan Walmsley were sent to the sin-bin two minutes later when a scuffle broke out and from the resulting penalty it was Haven that levelled the scores when Nikau Williams darted through a gap to score by the posts and Connor Holliday added the conversion. They went into the lead on twenty-four minutes when Holliday went over from close range and Walmsley this time added the conversion.

Cobi Green was also sent to the sin bin thirteen minutes from the break for holding down and while he was off Haven scored again when a bomb kick was launched towards the Lions line and Walmsley out jumped Jack Hansen to collect the ball and race away to score in the left corner, he also added the conversion to give them a twelve point advantage at the break.

Looking at how the Lions started the second half it looked like they had received the hair dryer treatment from Stuart Littler in the dressing room at the break. Paul Nash opened his Lions try scoring account when Ridyard sent him under the posts just after the restart and the conversion was added.

Two minutes later they were over again when Haven lost the ball in their own twenty and Mitch Cox raced in to score and Ridyard converted to level the scores. It got even better on fifty-one minutes when Ridyard engineered a try for Geronimo Doyle to score in the corner but the conversion attempt from the touchline sailed wide.

The scores were level again on sixty-four minutes when Walmsley added his second despite the efforts of Ben Heyes trying to knock him into touch but he missed the conversion from his own try. They again stretched into lead three minutes later when Karl Dixon went over and this was converted too and then with seven minutes left Holliday went through a fatigued defence to score by the posts, Walmsley again converted and the game was closed out in the last minute when the same player added a penalty goal from in front of the posts. It was a disappointment in the end for the large following of Lions fans.

Ian Rigg at the LEL Arena

Lions: Hansen, Roberts, Lloyd, Cox, Doyle, Ridyard, Green, Spencer, Waterworth, Meadows, Hope, Gregson, Brickhill. SUBS: J.Brown, Nash, T.Brown, Heyes

SWINTON LIONS BECOME ENGLAND TALENT PATHWAY ACCREDITED PARTNER
07 July 2021
Swinton Lions have been busy during the current lockdown, using the time to work on developing a player pathway to support both boys and girls towards the Lions first teams.

As part of this process they have successfully applied to the Rugby League to become an England Talent Pathway (ETP) Accredited Partner which focuses on players aged 12 – 16 based on the principles of open access and development of each individual.

RFL Talent Inclusion Manager Phil Jones was delighted with Swinton's application "Swinton have really worked hard on creating a clear plan for developing and supporting players. I am delighted to be able to accredit them as an ETP Partners as they have a real desire to develop children both on and off the field, some who may progress to a Performance level, others

who will continue playing socially or supporting the game"

"At Swinton Lions we are thrilled to have been officially approved as an England Talent Pathway Partner Club. Over the past 18 months, and despite the pandemic, we have been working hard on our long term strategic plan. We are putting structures in place that will enhance and underpin our relevance to the sport of rugby league for years to come, and it's a fantastic vote of confidence that our efforts and talented personnel are being officially recognised by our governing body.

"Being part of the England Talent Pathway programme, and implementing its aims and objectives, will attract talented youngsters to the club, and help put the building blocks in place to enable us create a genuine player pathway at Swinton Lions". Steve Wild, Operations Director.

VIKING JOINS LIONS ON LOAN
08 July 2021
We have agreed an initial two weeks loan deal with Widnes Vikings for Owen Buckley.

The 6 foot 4 inches winger is a local lad who progressed through the junior ranks at West Bank Bears and Halton Farnworth Hornets before joining the Widnes scholarship scheme at age 15. He went on to make a try-scoring Super League debut for the Vikings against Hull FC in 2018.
22 years old Owen will go straight into the Lions' squad for this Sunday's clash with Sheffield Eagles.
Welcome to Swinton, Owen!

SWINTON LIONS 22-30 SHEFFIELD EAGLES
12 July 2021

Eagles got back on the winning track but were made to fight for victory all the way right up until the last seconds of the game.

The Lions took the lead on five minutes after some good build up by Martyn Ridyard saw Rhodri Lloyd crash over on the right but the conversion attempt came back off the posts.

Eagles then tried to hit back and Rob Worrincy had a good chance down the right but some good tackles took him into touch, however they did hit back soon after when Ryan Millar went over on the left and Izaac Farrell converted to put them ahead. The Lions came back again when a loop pass from Cobi Green sent Owen Buckley over in the corner and Ridyard added the conversion.

It was the Eagles who started to look the stronger of the sides as half time approached and Aaron Brown went close only to be held up over the line and the Lions countered when Deane Meadows came onto a short pass near the line but lost control in the tackle.

Then came a double blow for the Lions defence when on the half hour Anthony Thackeray sent a super short pass to Ollie Davies and he raced away to score from thirty metres out and Farrell converted. Seven minutes later it was the same provider and the same scorer and they held an eight point lead at the break.

The second half started in the same way as the first had ended with the Eagles on the attack and Millar had a good chance but it took a good tackle from Buckley to stop his progress and the chance went.

Both defences were on top at this stage and they were cancelling out each others attacking play until Farrell put in a very nice short kick to the corner that bounced just right for Millar to pounce for his second but the conversion was missed by Farrell. Not long after he did add a penalty goal for obstruction to stretch the lead.

Millar completed his hat trick on sixty-six minutes when the ball bounced kindly for the winger to score in corner and Farrell again made no mistake with the conversion but it was the Lions who finished stronger. Firstly, Ben Heyes scored in the left corner after a good passing movement and then as the final hooter sounded Jack Hansen finished off a good move to dive in at the corner and Ridyard added the kick from the touchline.

Ian Rigg at Heywood Road

LIONS
7 Jack Hansen
38 Owen Buckley
11 Rhodri Lloyd
3 Mitch Cox
22 Geronimo Doyle
6 Martyn Ridyard
18 Cobi Green
39 Tom Spencer
9 Luke Waterworth
15 Louis Brogan
13 Will Hope
12 Nick Gregson
14 Billy Brickhill
Subs (all used)
21 Ben Heyes
24 Paul Nash
20 Tayler Brown
19 Deane Meadows

Tries: Lloyd (5), Buckley (16), Heyes (72), Hansen (80)
Goals: Ridyard ¾

EAGLES
Tries: Millar (13,58,66), Davies (31,38)
Goals: I.Farrell 5/6

LIONS APPOINT HEAD OF YOUTH DEVELOPMENT
13 July 2021

As the club continues to put structures in place to develop and support its wider strategic aims, and following the recent announcement that Swinton Lions was successful in receiving official RFL accreditation as an official England Talent Pathway partner, we are delighted to announce the appointment of our first ever Head of Youth Development.

The person taking up this historic and important role in the evolution of Swinton Lions is Dougie Owen, and he couldn't be better qualified! Dougie first joined the Lions in 2018 as an assistant coach, and over the past couple of years has led our Strength and Conditioning provision.

However, prior to joining Swinton, Dougie had already built up an impressive CV. In 2013 he joined the Development Programme and Scholarship Team at Wigan Warriors, a position he held for 5 years. During that period another couple of milestones were achieved, as in 2014 he became first person to be accredited as an England Talent Pathway Coach for the RFL.

Then a year later Dougie was awarded the RFL's prestigious 'Juniors Coach of the Year' award. In addition, Dougie has worked as a Coach Developer for the RFL, and has delivered England Talent Pathway training to Community Coaches for both the RFL and Wigan Warriors. He also spent time as the Strength and Conditioning Coach for the England Community Lions.

Upon his appointment **Dougie** said, "This is not only a fantastic opportunity for me to get to work with talented players and coaches in the local area, but also an honour to be offered the position with a club of Swinton Lions' standing. I will do everything possible to match the drive and determination of the club to build something special. I'd like to thank the Board for their confidence in me, and Stu Littler for his continual support."

Lions' CEO **Steve Wild** added, "Dougie's impressive CV speaks for itself. But his passion for the club, and for developing and helping players, not to mention his passion for the sport of Rugby League in general, is something that you can't bottle. We feel very fortunate at Swinton to have someone of Dougie's drive and energy committing to this important role as we look to underpin our broader strategic aims. But on top of all that, in Dougie you couldn't wish to meet a nicer person, and he is perfect for the role."

IRISH INTERNATIONAL RONAN MICHAEL RE-JOINS LIONS
22 July 2021

We are delighted to announce the re-signing of Irish international forward Ronan Michael, who joins the Lions for the remainder of the 2021 season.

The former Dublin Longhorns player comes to us from Huddersfield Giants, to whom we extend our grateful thanks for their assistance in arranging the Loan.

20 years old Ronan has already appeared twice for Swinton this season, and greatly impressed on our visits to Batley in the league, and in scoring a try at York City Knights in the 1895 Cup semi-final.

We are sure Swinton Lions fans will be pleased at this news, and will join us in welcoming Ronan back to the club.

TRIALIST BEN STEELE LINKS UP WITH LIONS
23 July 2021

We have signed on trialist forms the former Salford Academy, Manchester Rangers and London

Skolars utility-back, Ben Steele.

Ben who has been playing at Coffs Harbour in Australia, recently returned to the UK and was looking to return to the professional game.

After a recommendation from the Manchester Rangers Foundation as a player who could really flourish in a professional environment, and following video analysis, we offered Ben a one month trial period.

MATCH REPORT – YORK CITY KNIGHTS 46 SWINTON LIONS 10
26 July 2021

A much-changed Lions side suffered a heavy defeat in the Yorkshire sunshine.

The Knights took the lead straight from the kick-off when Kieran Dixon's kick bounced very unkindly forcing Owen Buckley to catch the ball but he fell into touch as he caught it. From the play the ball, Chris Clarkson crossed for the opening try after only fifty-six seconds but Dixon was off target with the conversion attempt.

The second try came after seven minutes when birthday boy Ronan Dixon went over by the posts and Kieran Dixon converted. Three minutes later it got even worse when Leeds Rhinos academy prospect Corey Hall made a super break down the left to feed the supporting Dixon and he raced over and added the conversion to his own try.

The Lions hit back on twenty-two minutes when Jack Hansen launched a kick down field and Dixon collected it in his own twenty but the chasing Hansen stole the ball one on one in the tackle and this attack finished with Ben Heyes scoring in the left corner. Hansen could not add the conversion from the touchline.

The Lions had a couple of good attacking sets after this with Ronan Michael and Mitch Cox going close but it was the Knights who increased their lead seven minutes from the break when Matty Marsh opened the defence to set up Danny Kirmond and Dixon converted this one. Another Lions chance was blown just before the break when Buckley rose higher than Dixon to collect a high kick and pass to the supporting Luis Roberts but the pass was forward and the Knights held an eighteen point lead at the break.

Defences were on top early in the second half and it was the Lions who scored first when Deane Meadows crossed by the posts on fifty-two minutes and Hansen added the conversion. Play then got a little sloppy with both teams making many handling errors before Marsh sold a dummy to score by the posts and Dixon converted.

Hansen created a little bit of magic on sixty-five minutes when he chipped the Knights defence and regathered the ball before putting a kick to the corner for the chasing Ben Heyes but the ball just over ran him. Luis Roberts had to leave the field on sixty-seven minutes for a head check and he didn't return. The Knights finished strongly scoring three more tries in the final twelve minutes with Marsh, Dixon and Dow-Nikau all going over and Dixon converting them all.

Ian Rigg at the LNER Community Stadium

Lions: Doyle, Buckley, Roberts, Cox, Heyes, Green, Hansen, Spencer, Waterworth, Michael, Hope, Gregson, Brogan. Subs : J.Brown, Jones, Nash, Meadows.

CLUB UPDATE – HEYWOOD ROAD GROUND ADMISSION & MATCH DAY PROTOCOL
28 July 2021

Following the Government's recent relaxation of Covid regulations, we would like to provide our supporters with an update in respect of match day attendance at Heywood Road.

We are of course mindful that the Government and the RFL is advising a cautious approach, and that is reflected in our revised Spectator Communications Plan.

Moving forward we will of course continue to provide an online ticketing facility, but as of the match against Oldham on 8th August 2021, we will also revert to allowing cash payments on the main gate.

We are also pleased to confirm that the Downstairs (Steve Smith) Bar will revert to its intended use as of 8th August, with the Away Team no longer utilising it as a dressing room. Our Supporters' Trust merchandise stall will also be operational once more in the Downstairs Bar. However, for the time being, we would ask bar users to follow the one-way system in operation and not congregate indoors. Instead please take drinks from the Downstairs Bar outside to consume.

In respect of the Upstairs Bar, we still need to control numbers, albeit with a more relaxed approach. Corporate Diners, Club Guests, and 2020 Season Ticket Holders will be welcome to utilise the Upstairs Bar. However, whilst we intend to continue with table service for the time being, which is partly designed to assist our staff, it will now be possible to take your drinks outside. However, all drinks to be consumed outside, obtained from either bar, should be in a plastic container.

2020 Season Ticket Holders (full donators or partial donators) will be able to collect their ticket from the Trust's Merchandise Stall on 8th August, and then use it to access the Upstairs Bar. Pre-bookings will no longer be necessary for those supporters who qualify for Upstairs Bar access.

Please note that the "Red Zone" for players, match officials and coaching/backroom staff will remain operative, so please bear this in mind when communicating with our stewards and club staff who may need to restrict access to particular areas at certain times.

LIONS PART COMPANY WITH STUART LITTLER
29 July 2021

Swinton Lions RLFC can confirm that it has parted company with Head Coach Stuart Littler.

The Board wishes to acknowledge that Stuart Littler has been an outstanding servant to Swinton Lions over the past 6 years. He is a top-quality coach and a thoroughly decent human being. This season Stuart has had to contend with an unprecedented injury list, but we are in a results driven business, and the Board felt that the time had come for a fresh approach.

We are sure that all Swinton fans will join us in thanking Stuart for his service, professionalism and work ethic, as we wish him nothing but the best in the future.

Assistant Coach Allan Coleman has agreed take over first team affairs until the end of the 2021 season, at which point the Head Coach position will be reviewed.

August

MATCH REPORT – DEWSBURY RAMS 18-22 SWINTON LIONS
02 August 2021

Swinton's season finally got off the mark with a dramatic victory in the dying seconds when Paul Sykes was going for a drop goal to win the game, but the ball bounced off Jack Hansen and he dribbled it up

field to score in the corner as the final hooter sounded.

The Lions made a strong start and had a chance in the opening two minutes but it was brought back for a forward pass, however they did take the lead three minutes later when a good passage of play saw Rhodri Lloyd send his winger Owen Buckley swallow diving into the corner to score the opening try but Jack Hansen could not convert from the touchline.

From the restart Mitch Cox knocked on putting his side under pressure but the defence held out. Rams took the lead on nineteen minutes, and this too came from a Lions attack that broke down in the Rams ten with Matt Fleming scooping up Cobi Green's kick to race eighty metres to score despite a great effort by Louis Brogan to knock him into touch and Paul Sykes added the conversion.

It got better for the home side twelve minutes from the break when some good pressure on the line saw Jon Magrin crash over by the posts and Sykes added the simple conversion. It was the Rams who finished the half stronger trying to capitalise on some Lions errors with the ball, but the defence held.

Rams had a player put on report in the opening minute of the second half for a possible crush tackle on Deane Meadows, but it was the home side who stretched the lead when Sam Day went over from close range on forty-three minutes and Sykes again converted. The Lions messed up again from the restart and this allowed a chance for Andy Gabriel but it took a great tackle by Mike Butt to stop him scoring.

Tempers were starting to boil, and Rhodri Lloyd was sent to the sin bin for a late attack on Day and then three minutes later Sykes was sent to the sin bin for an attack on Lewis Hatton. The Lions then hit a purple patch when Hansen took control to firstly create a try for Brogan who went in by the posts and Hansen converted and then on fifty-five minutes, he created one for Mitch Cox converting this one too.

Rams then tried to fight back but Chris Annakin was held up and Joe Martin sailed through a gap only to be brought back for obstruction in the build-up. The Lions forced a goal line drop out five minutes from time and a minute later Will Hope was hit off the ball dead centre of field thirty metres out and Hansen added the penalty conversion to level the scores at 18-18.

Then came the drama in the dying minutes when firstly Sykes tried to win it with a couple of drop goal attempts but the second one hit Hansen and propelled past the Rams defence for Hansen to dribble to the line and score in the corner with the large following of Lions fans going ecstatic on the terraces, Hansen then missed the conversion but it didn't really matter.

Ian Rigg at The Tetley's Stadium
LIONS
22 Geronimo Doyle
38 Owen Buckley
11 Rhodri Lloyd
3 Mitch Cox
1 Mike Butt
7 Jack Hansen
18 Cobi Green
16 Paddy Jones
9 Luke Waterworth
10 Lewis Hatton
15 Louis Brogan
12 Nick Gregson
13 Will Hope
Subs (all used)
19 Deane Meadows
40 Ronan Michael
39 Tom Spencer
24 Paul Nash

Tries: Buckley (4), Brogan (52), Cox (55), Hansen (80)
Goals: Hansen 3/5

Post Match Comments from Steve Wild

On Thursday we parted company with Stuart Littler as head coach of Swinton Lions, but I want to say it was by far the toughest decision we've ever had to take since taking control of the club. Stuart is a top class bloke who gave everything to this club for over 6 years, and on a personal level I have nothing but respect for him. Even on Thursday he handled himself with the utmost dignity.

Stuart came to us in 2015 when John Duffy was head coach , and was an integral member of our team that got to the ipro cup final and then won promotion to the Championship.

He later became assistant coach , and when Duffs left in July 2017, and in the midst of the financial meltdown following the departure of the then chairman, myself and Alan Marshall appointed Stu as head coach. It was the most torrid of times, and we came very very close to losing the club completely, but Stu held things together with the players and staff whilst we could concentrate on saving the company off it.

Against all the odds we pulled off an incredible win at Odsal against Bradford , then after winning at Dewsbury we won the Million Penny game against Oldham to stay in the Championship.

2018 was a difficult season as a lot of rebuilding was required, but we ended up beating Workington in a play-off game to retain our Championship status. Things improved in 2019 and we ended up in our highest league position in two decades under Stuart's leadership.

Myself and Stuart then had the problem of steadying the ship again in autumn of 2019 when the majority of the board resigned . We were back under the spotlight again , with the RFL placing us in special measures due to the sudden uncertainties surrounding the club. Again against difficult circumstances Stuart held things together with the players and staff, and we set about restructuring our off-field operations . I worked closely with Stu as we started to build for the 2020 season. Stuart understood the restrictions we had to work under , but he fully understood where we were , never complained , and just got on with doing his best for the club.

Then came covid and all the challenges we faced as a result of that . The red tape was a minefield, but again Stuart diligently continued to do his absolute best with the players , even though he was very restricted in what he was able to do because of covid regulations .

Into 2021 and the most horrendous run of injuries I can ever remember at the club. Still Stuart battled on, and refused to let injuries be an excuse for our results. But sadly it eventually came to a point where we had to consider if a fresh approach was the right way forward for the club.

From the bottom of my heart , thank you Stuart Littler for everything you did for our club . You will always be a Lion , and you'll always be welcome at Swinton , and we wish you all the very best in the future.

Follow Up Comments from Stuart Fletcher

I would just like to concur with everything Steve has said.

A big thank you to Stu for everything he has done for this club and will always be a Lions legend. A pleasure working with Stu.

A hugely respected coach within the game but equally if not more important a fantastic person who has integrity and honesty as values.

As Steve said a very difficult decision and wish Stu the very best for the future and always welcome at the Lions.

SPENCER RETURNS TO LEIGH
02 August 2021
We can confirm that Tom Spencer's loan deal has come to an end, and the player has now returned to his parent club Leigh Centurions.

We would like to place on record our thanks to Tom personally for all his efforts in a Swinton shirt, culminating in yesterday's victory at Dewsbury, as well as thank Leigh Centurions for their co operation in arranging the loan.

In other club news, we can confirm that Sam Grant has departed Swinton Lions for personal reasons. Again we'd like to thank Sam for all his efforts for the Lions, and we wish him well for the future.

SWINTON LIONS 22-22 OLDHAM
09 August 2021
Both teams went home with a point each in this pulsating end to end game which Swinton almost stole at the end.

Oldham made the brighter start and Dan Abram almost got Danny Bridge over on the first attack, but the ball went to ground. They then lost Liam Kirk to a head injury who didn't return to the field and likewise the Lions lost Owen Buckley who appeared to catch a stray boot in the tackle. Oldham started to turn the screw as the half wore on and some poor tackling allowed Tyler Dupree to break the line and score under the posts with Dan Abram converting which was quickly followed by Bridge going over but this was brought back for a forward pass.

The Lions had a glorious chance on twenty-six minutes but a final pass to Mike Butt failed to find the flyer and the ball went into touch. Within a minute Oldham scored again when Dupree broke tackles again to score by the posts and Abram converted. It was the Lions who made the stronger finish to the half forcing a goal line drop out and some handling errors, but they could not capitalise.

It was a bad start to the second half for the Lions when they lost Jack Hansen to a back injury in the first minute and he did not return so the team had to re-shuffle. This seemed to work instantly, and it was Martyn Ridyard who sent out a lovely short pass that Lewis Hatton came on too nicely to score under the posts with Ridyard converting. However, from the restart Oldham forced the Lions into a goal line drop out and Lloyd Roby finished off a nice move to score in the left corner, but Abram missed the conversion.

The Lions were not for lying down and Hatton went over for a second on fifty-three minutes after a nice pass from Sam Brooks and this time Nick Gregson converted. Within nine minutes Swinton were in the lead when Ridyard, Will Hope and Mitch Cox all combined to send Butt in at the corner and Ridyard added a superb kick from the touchline.

Dupree was held up by the Lions defence fourteen minutes from time and from the close play the ball Lewis Charnock put in a short kick to the line and James Barran won the race to score to the right of the posts with Abram converting to give Oldham back the lead.

Again it was the Lions who came alive in the final ten minutes and they had a few chances on the line before Dupree was sent to the sin-bin for a shoulder charge. With four minutes to go and from the penalty pressure the Lions threw the ball around and it was Ridyard and Rhodri Lloyd who combined to send part time winger Deane Meadows over on the right to level the scores but the conversion from Ridyard just sailed to the right of the posts. It was all down to the last minute and Oldham had a glorious chance to snatch the game in the dying seconds but the drop goal attempt from Barran sailed wide.

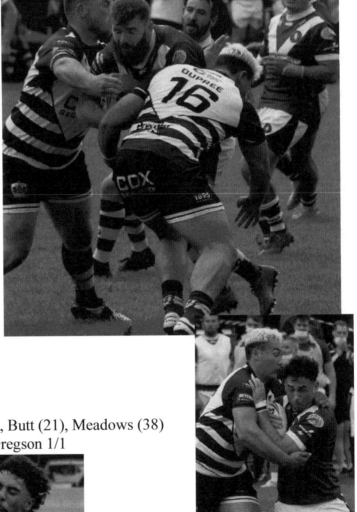

LIONS
22 Geronimo Doyle
37 Owen Buckley
3 Mitch Cox
11 Rhodri Lloyd
1 Mike Butt
6 Martyn Ridyard
7 Jack Hansen
16 Paddy Jones
9 Luke Waterworth
10 Lewis Hatton
12 Nick Gregson
15 Louis Brogan
13 Will Hope
Subs (all used)
8 Sam Brooks
40 Ronan Michael
24 Paul Nash
19 Deane Meadows
Tries: Hatton (44,53), Butt (21), Meadows (38)
Goals: Ridyard 2/3 Gregson 1/1

SWINTON LIONS 6-38 BATLEY BULLDOGS
16 August 2021

Batley substitute Alistair Leak scored a hat-trick to help his side to an

impressive victory over Swinton Lions in Round 17 of the Betfred Championship.

The home side were given a blow in the warm up when Sam Brooks pulled up and had to be replaced by Jordan Brown.

The Lions made a good start and forced a goal line drop out on six minutes, but Martyn Ridyard lost the ball in a good position with the Lions on the attack from the kick. However, Swinton did take the lead on nine minutes when Ridyard put a short kick for the line and Luis Roberts reacted quickest to dive on the rolling ball and Ridyard added the conversion from near the touchline.

After that the game settled and both sides had good chances before the Bulldogs opened their account on twenty-eight minutes when Jonny Campbell went over on the right but Tom Gilmore could not convert. Batley were in again seven minutes later when George Senior took three defenders with him to score in the corner with this time Gilmore adding a touchline conversion.

Leak was starting to make his mark in the closing minutes of the half and almost scored but knocked on just short of the line. As the half time hooter sounded Gilmore sent a nice kick towards the Lions line and Campbell this time was fastest to react beating the Lions defence to the rolling ball and Gilmore rubbed more salt in the Lions wounds by adding the conversion from the touchline.

The visitors continued at the start of the second half as they had left the first and it was Leak who scored on the first attack when he stripped the ball one on one off Geronimo Doyle to race away to score under the posts and Gilmore converted.

The Lions tried to come back again but some great Bulldogs defence held them out and they were rewarded for their efforts again when Dale Morton almost scored but was stopped by a great tackle by Mike Butt. From the resulting play the ball the lively hooker went over from acting half back and Gilmore again converted. Ben Heyes went close for the Lions on the hour, but again good defence managed to hold him out.

Bulldogs scored again with sixteen minutes left when Greg Johnson intercepted a loose Lions carry to race away up field only to be grounded short and from the play the ball Gilmore created a try for the flyer to dive in at the corner. With five minutes left it was Leak who scored his third try going over from close range again and Gilmore added the conversion to complete a good afternoon for his team.

LIONS
22 Geronimo Doyle
1 Mike Butt
11 Rhodri Lloyd
25 Luis Roberts
21 Ben Heyes
6 Martyn Ridyard
18 Cobi Green
40 Ronan Michael
9 Luke Waterworth
10 Lewis Hatton
3 Mitch Cox
12 Nick Gregson
15 Louis Brogan
Subs (all used)
14 Billy Brickhill
16 Paddy Jones
26 Jordan Brown
20 Tayler Brown
Try: Roberts (9)
Goal: Ridyard 1/1

Above: Former Swinton Secretary and all-round club legend Steve Moyse presents a souvenir Lions shirt to our Headline Match Sponsor Paul Albert of Viking Excavations and Civils Ltd. A big thank you to everyone at Viking for your extremely generous support!

Right: Steve presents a signed Swinton ball to our Match Ball Sponsor Sam Collier. A big thank you to Sam and wife Anne for your ongoing support!

BRADFORD BULLS 30-26 SWINTON LIONS

24 August 2021
Braford Bulls were given a huge fright by bottom side Swinton Lions and could have even either drawn or lost the game in the dying seconds when Louis Brogan went so close only to lose the

ball near the line on the last play of the game.

In the first 15 minutes both sides tested each other's defences, but it was the Bulls who exploited the first gap when Brandon Pickersgill was on the end of a huge overlap to score on the left and Jordan Lilley converted. The Lions almost hit back on twenty-two minutes when Lewis Hatton should have scored under the posts but couldn't hold the pass with the line open.

Bulls then went straight down field to add their second when David Foggin-Johnson broke down the left and gave the ball to the supporting Pickersgill who fed Ross Oakes to juggle his way to the line to score and Lilley again converted.

The Lions hit back on twenty-six minutes when Luis Roberts followed a kick to the corner which the Bulls defence couldn't control so the winger dived in for the try but Jack Hansen was unable to convert. It then got even better for the visitors when the Bulls were on the attack down the right and Joe Brown threw out a long pass which fell behind all his attackers and was swept up by Lions winger Ben Heyes who raced seventy metres to score under the posts and Nick Gregson converted to put his side within two points.

The Lions made a strong start to the second half and almost scored on their first attack when Luke Waterworth was held up over the line thanks to some good defence. Martyn Ridyard kicked a twenty-forty on forty-three minutes, but his side were unable to capitalise with the ball.

George Flanagan had been introduced to the field just before the break and he went close three minutes into the second half, but the livewire hooker did get on the scoreboard on fifty-two minutes when he darted over by the posts after the Lions lost the ball and Lilley converted. Four minutes later he repeated with another dart this time from acting half after Lilley went close and again Lilley converted to give his side a fourteen point lead. Again, the Lions came back on the hour when a long cut out pass saw Roberts go over in the corner for his second, but Ridyard could not convert this one.

Matty Dawson-Jones went close on the right before Foggin-Johnson put more daylight on the scoreboard when he cut inside to score under the posts and Lilley again made no mistake with the boot.

The Lions were not lying down and with nine minutes left Hansen chipped the Bulls defence and then hacked the ball towards the line and Rhodri Lloyd followed the kick which bounced up nicely for him to score under the posts and Ridyard converted to narrow the lead. It got even better with two minutes left when Cobi Green was fouled as he sent up a high kick towards the line and from the resulting penalty ten metres out Ridyard went through the Bulls defence to score by the posts, he also added the conversion to bring his side within four points and set up a grandstand finish. With seconds to go to the hooter the Lions were on the attack and Louis Brogan broke a couple of tackles but as he went for glory he lost control of the ball as the hooter sounded and it was a huge relief for the Bulls.

BULLS
Tries: Pickersgill (15), Oakes (23), Flanagan (52,55), Foggin-Johnson (66)
Goals: Lilley 5/5
LIONS
22 Geronimo Doyle
25 Luis Roberts
11 Rhodri Lloyd
1 Mike Butt
21 Ben Heyes
6 Martyn Ridyard
7 Jack Hansen
8 Sam Brooks
9 Luke Waterworth
10 Lewis Hatton
3 Mitch Cox
12 Nick Gregson

15 Louis Brogan
Subs (all Used)
14 Billy Brickhill
40 Ronan Michael
16 Paddy Jones
18 Cobi Green
Tries: Roberts (26,59), Heyes (29), Lloyd (70), Ridyard (77)
Goals: Hansen 0/1
Gregson 1/1
Ridyard 2/3

HAMLETT JOINS SWINTON UNTIL THE END OF THE SEASON
27 August 2021
We are pleased to
announce that Bradford
Bulls winger or centre
Reece Hamlett has joined
the Lions on loan for the
remainder of the season.

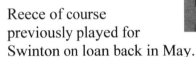

Reece of course
previously played for
Swinton on loan back in May.
We'd like to thank all concerned at the Bulls for facilitating the loan
agreement.

LIONS CONFIRM ALLAN COLEMAN AS HEAD COACH
28 August 2021
Swinton Lions RLFC
can confirm that
former Assistant
Coach Allan
Coleman, who was
recently placed in
temporary charge until
the end of the current
season, has now been
formally appointed as
Head Coach until at
least the end of the
2022 campaign.

Before joining the Lions as Stuart Littler's assistant ahead of the 2019 season, Allan had previously enjoyed a highly successful coaching career with Leigh Miners Rangers in the National Conference League, and has also enjoyed success with the England Community Lions.

Upon his official confirmation, **Allan** said, "I am very honoured to be asked to become Head Coach at Swinton Lions. I have loved my time here so far and I can't wait to lead this great club. Firstly I would like to thank the Board for giving me this opportunity, and also thank the players and staff who have been brilliant since I was initially asked to step up a few weeks ago. We now need to give the fans something to cheer about again and a team to be proud of, and that's a main priority. The other top priority is to build a squad for 2022 and we already getting on with that. As the saying goes, 'Once a Lion always a Lion'!"

Lions' CEO **Steve Wild** said, "Allan's confirmation as Head Coach was an easy decision for the Board to make. He has a great rapport with the players and staff, and not only has this been reflected in recent performances, but also on the training field. He's honed his coaching career at the highest levels in the community game, including at international standard, and we have every confidence that he'll now do a terrific job at semi-professional level with Swinton. Allan has been at the club for almost three years now, and as well as being a highly respected coach he understands and buys into the ethos of our club. Admittedly we've had a terrible year with injuries and as a consequence it looks like we'll have to take a temporary step back before we can take two forward. But we remain a highly ambitious club and we believe Allan is the man to take us on the next exciting steps of our journey. There are some tough challenges ahead for all clubs, but at Swinton Lions we are aiming for a successful 2022 on the field, whilst continuing to enhance our profile off it. I think this will be a popular appointment with our fans, and I'm sure they'll give Allan their 100% support."

HALIFAX PANTHERS 48-12 SWINTON LIONS
29 August 2021
The Panthers got their season back on track with a mauling of the Lions scoring some excellent tries to keep them well in the play off hunt.

Connor Robinson almost opened the scoring in the early minutes after some good play by Greg Worthington, however the Lions almost hit back with Luis Roberts going away to score after intercepting a pass but there had been a knock on in the build-up.

The Panthers' first score came on eight minutes when Matt Garside broke clear to send Brandon Moore away to score by the posts and Robinson converted. There was another Lions  attack that came to nothing before Moore added his second again scoring under the posts after good play by Scott Grix and Dan Murray with Robinson adding the conversion.

This was quickly followed by a well created try by Grix down the right for James Saltonstall who scored in the corner, but Robinson could not convert this one. Panthers were capitalising on Swinton's handling errors and another lost ball saw Ben Kavanagh race away to score on the left and Robinson again was on target with his kick. On the last play of the half Jacob Fairbank was this time the provider when Liam Harris raced in on the left but the conversion was missed.

Simon Grix's half time team talk would have been straight forward more of the same but the Lions reshuffled during the break and they made a strong start keeping the Panthers defence pinned on their line for several sets before Rhodri Lloyd found his way over to the right of the posts and this was converted by Martyn Ridyard. They continued this assault on the Panthers line but were unable to break through before Ridyard put up a high kick towards the line and the ball came down to Reece Hamlett who found Will Hope to score under the posts with Ridyard converting. The Panthers then got back on track on sixty-one minutes when Garside scored by the posts and Robinson converted again.

There were then a few chances for both sides but great defence from both with Lloyd being held up for the Lions and Grix, Curtis Davies and Adam Tangata for the Panthers before Ben Tibbs scored after a good passing movement down the left, but this went unconverted and was quickly followed with three minutes to go when Grix got his deserved try and Robinson converted again.

There was a grandstand finish to the game with the Lions getting a penalty as the hooter sounded but as they moved the ball to the right a Lions player was taken out and another penalty was awarded by referee Nick Bennett. The Lions played the ball and moved it swiftly to the left and Jack Hansen tried to kick through the Panthers defence but the ball bounced nicely for Zack McComb who raced full length of the field to score, and Robinson converted to end a perfect day for his side.

Ian Rigg at The Shay Stadium

PANTHERS
Tries: Moore (8,13), Saltonstall (17), Kavanagh (27), Harris (39), Garside (61), Tibbs (76), Grix (77), McComb (80)
Goals: Robinson 6/9

LIONS
7 Jack Hansen
22 Geronimo Doyle
1 Mike Butt
39 Reece Hamlett
25 Luis Roberts
6 Martyn Ridyard
18 Cobi Green
13 Will Hope
9 Luke Waterworth
10 Lewis Hatton
11 Rhodri Lloyd
3 Mitch Cox
15 Louis Brogan
Subs (all used)
14 Billy Brickhill
24 Paul Nash
16 Paddy Jones
40 Ronan Michael
Tries:
Lloyd (44), Hope (57)
Goals: Ridyard 2/2

LIONESSES EARN INTERNATIONAL RECOGNITION!
31 August 2021

At Swinton Lions we are proud and thrilled to announce that just six months after forming our female teams, two of our "Lionesses" have been selected at international level, with both Maddie Corrigan and Holly Grimes being brought into the Ireland train-on squad for 2021 and 2022.

It is great testament to the training regime being put in place by our Lionesses coaches Martina Greenwood and Steve Thirkell, as well of course the hard work and commitment of Holly and Maddie themselves, that Swinton is already being looked at as a source of potential international talent.

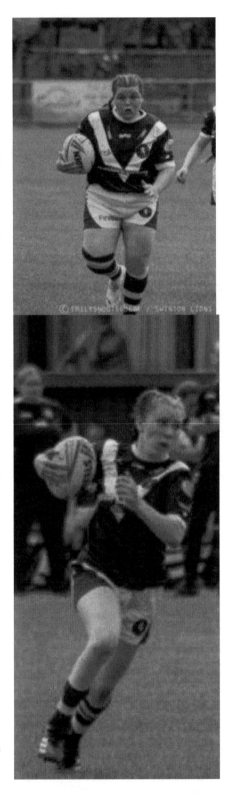

Holly Grimes will already be known to many of our supporters, as she and her family were already keen Lions' fans even before the formation of the Lionesses. This is her first season playing Rugby League, although she did have some previous experience playing the Union code. Upon her selection for the Ireland squad, **Holly**, a forward, said, "It's a thrill to achieve recognition in such a big sport, and being able to represent not only my club but also my family is a great honour. When my name was selected out of all those that trialled, it showed me that the blood, sweat and tears over the years have been worth it in the end."

Maddison Corrigan is a strong running centre who came to Swinton following 12 months at Leigh East. Maddie is a player who is always looking to learn and develop. and she has adapted well to play in both the Lionesses Under 16s and Open Age teams at Swinton. She is a very bright 16-year-old emerging talent and definitely one to watch in the future. **Maddie** said, "I am so thrilled to make the squad. My family have very strong Irish heritage and it means a lot to both my family and myself to represent Ireland. I have worked hard whilst playing and training for Swinton and can honestly say it's the best feeling being one of the first ever Swinton Lionesses to gain recognition at this level. However, the hardest works begins now and I cannot wait for it!"

Everyone at the club, including all of their team mates in the Lionesses, are immensely proud of Holly and Maddie, and we feel that this is only the beginning for both girls as well as for the rest of the Swinton Lionesses!

September
SWINTON LIONS 32-34 LONDON BRONCOS
06 September 2021
The Broncos might have got the two points, but they will know they were in a contest after a fantastic second half fight back by the Lions.

It was a bad start for both sides as both teams were unable to hold the ball for the first three sets of the game, but the Lions capitalised on the Broncos second set when they lost the ball and some pressure saw Jack Hansen go over on the right, Martyn Ridyard was unable to convert.

It got even better for the Lions on ten minutes when Lewis Hatton ran onto a nice short pass to score under the posts and Ridyard this time converted.

James Meadows then set up a try for Greg Richards who touched down by the posts and Chris Hankinson converted for London's first score of the game.

Broncos took the lead on nineteen minutes when Pat Moran scored by the posts after a penalty was given away by Sam Brooks for a shoulder off the ball and Hankinson converted to put his side ahead.

The Lions went back into the lead on twenty-six minutes when Ridyard scored after a kind bounce and also converted but again this did not last long as the Broncos came back strongly with Abbas Miski scoring in the corner again converted by Hankinson from the touch line. It got better for the visitors as they ran in two more tries in a three minute period with Sadiq Adebiyi and Gideon Boafo both going over before the break with Hankinson converting one of them to give his side a twelve point advantage at half-time. The Lions started much better after the break, Luke Waterworth had a great effort in the early minutes but again the ball just went away with the line open and then Boafo added his second try after some good build up by Dan Hindmarsh with Hankinson again converting.

The Lions were playing the better rugby in the second half and Ronan Michael went close just before a good break by Rhodri Lloyd which set up a try under the posts for the supporting Mike Butt and Ridyard converted.

Lloyd then pulled off a try saving tackle on Tuoyo Egodo before Ridyard set up a try for Ben Heyes with a measured kick for the corner that the winger won the race to score and Ridyard converted off the touchline.

There were six points in it with twelve minutes to go and the Lions had chance after chance but some good defence by the Broncos held them out with Butt, Mitch Cox and Billy Brickhill all going close. Eventually the defence was breached when Luis Roberts crashed over in the right corner but the touchline conversion attempt from Ridyard landed just to the right of the posts and with two minutes left it looked like Geronimo Doyle had snatched the victory but he was held up as he went for the left corner.

Ian Rigg at Heywood Road

LIONS
22 Geronimo Doyle
21 Ben Heyes
1 Mike Butt
39 Reece Hamlett
25 Luis Roberts
6 Martyn Ridyard
7 Jack Hansen
8 Sam Brooks
9 Luke Waterworth
10 Lewis Hatton
11 Rhodri Lloyd
3 Mitch Cox
14 Billy Brickhill
Subs (all used)
12 Nick Gregson
15 Louis Brogan
13 Will Hope
40 Ronan Michael

Tries: Hansen (4), Hatton (10), Ridyard (26), Butt (57), Heyes (66), Roberts (77)
Goals: Ridyard 4/6

BRONCOS
Tries: Richards (16), Moran (19), Miski (29), Adebiyi (32), Boafo (35,51),
Goals: 5/6

OBITUARY – MIKE PEERS
08 September 2021

Mike Peers joined the Lions in September 1981 from hometown club Warrington for whom he had made 55 first team appearances. Mike was a "players' player", operating as a natural loose forward. Mike had the lot, a good rugby brain, great hands, sidestep and an astute kicking game.

Mike's natural skills encompassed leadership and man management. As the Lions' 'A' Team player coach his contribution was pivotal in the lead up to the club's halcyon season of 1986/87. By then appointed joint first team coach with Bill Holliday, the Lions took the inaugural Second Division Premiership Trophy played at Old Trafford against Hunslet, and also won promotion to the First Division.

Mike's humour was wicked! Picture this. Swinton 'A' were away to Carlisle at Penrith in the bleak midwinter and we had been reassured that the pitch was playable. On arrival, Mike, myself and the three match officials slipped and slithered towards the centre spot where you could almost see your reflection in the frost and ice. With the straightest of faces Mike said, "Who has declared this match on? Torville and Dean?" We were on our way home within ten minutes.

Mike Peers didn't need a CV – just ask the players he played with and coached. For myself and so many it was a true privilege to have shared a small part of Mike's life as a colleague and a friend.
A young lad who grew to love the game and it's people, who in turn loved him for the very same reasons.

"Farewell old friend, the game is o'er, the whistle's blown, the flag we lower."

Say not in grief he is no more, but in thankfulness he was.

Mike Peers played 37 games, and scored 5 tries and 3 goals for the Lions. But these statistics are a mere drop in the ocean, his contribution to rugby league and to our club was a tsunami.

Mike Peers RIP

The club would like to thank Steve Moyse for preparing these words.

Open Fans Meeting
9th September 2021
The club held an open forum at the Royal British Legion, Cheetham Road, Swinton and Steve Wild produced the following report:

Following the open fans' meeting on Thursday night I began to prepare some summary notes, with the intention that they would also double as my programme column for next Sunday's match against Widnes. However, for the benefit of those that were not able to attend on Thursday , I'm copying the notes below.

Obviously if I repeated every word that was said on Thursday, this post would be ridiculously long, so therefore if anyone has any questions whatsoever, just ask on this thread and we will do our best to answer. If you'd rather ask a question in private, send an email to myself, Stuart or Damian (or all 3 of us).

Whilst admittedly there is always scope to improve on such matters as comms (and we will always happily take any constructive criticism on board), I also believe that accusations of "secret society" are a million miles from the actual truth. There seems to be an assumption in some quarters that we hold a big bag of secrets - we don't - and only a very few matters of extreme sensitivity, which would otherwise damage the club if released, are kept close to hand. The chairman has frequently delivered podcasts over recent weeks covering a multitude of subjects, plus we try to produce newsworthy items on a frequent basis for our social media outlets.

The sport is about to go through a seismic change, and we are doing everything possible to protect our club, your club, and give it sustainable foundations for the future. That process is made a lot easier with a united front.

"Welcome to our final home game of the 2021 season here at Heywood Road.

As well as welcoming our guests from Widnes Vikings, I would like, on behalf of the Board, to thank all of our volunteers, sponsors, partners, and supporters, plus of course our stadium hosts Sale FC, for all of your help, co operation and dedication through what has been a pretty tough year. This of course has culminated in a disappointing season on the field, one which is likely to see us relegated, against the backdrop of the most horrendous injury list I can ever remember at this club. However, please be rest assured that despite the enormous challenges faced by the sport as a whole, we are already in advanced on-field planning for 2022, and it's absolutely our intention to come back bigger and stronger than ever.

Ten days ago at Swinton British Legion, the Board, supported by Head Coach Allan Coleman and team captain Rhodri Lloyd, presented a club update to our fans. I really hope that those of you who attended were able to take on board a couple of key messages. Firstly, and despite results in 2021, the club is in a stable situation both on and off the field, but secondly it is inevitable that we are going to need your help even more than ever if we are to plot a long term sustainable and successful future for Swinton Lions.

To summarise the British Legion meeting, Rhodri Lloyd delivered a heartfelt message on behalf of the players, and held both hands up for a poor season of results on the field in 2021. However, this was coupled with an assurance that the lads will be going all out to make amends in 2022. Allan Coleman then spoke very eloquently about the pride in his recent appointment, and of his determination to develop a squad around players that  buy into the ethos of our club, and will be willing to run through a brick wall for it.

I then personally spoke about the journey from 2019 to date, of the many challenges we have negotiated as a business, including the governance and restructuring of the club, its financial and ownership stability, and of course our success in getting through covid. But also I presented a note of caution regarding the need to align ourselves effectively to face the challenges ahead following the next broadcasting deal and dramatic reduction in central funding. Chairman Stuart Fletcher then dealt with those issues specifically arising from the current season, particularly on the playing side, and of the recent appointment of Allan Coleman. Finally Damian Ridpath, our Development Director, spoke passionately about the enormous progress being made off the field, particularly in respect of the incredibly successful relaunch of our Lions' Foundation, which has resulted in a huge increase in community engagement via our Swinton Lionesses and Manchester Lions programmes, and the importance of the club being confirmed as an England Talent Pathway partner.

Overall it was a united but simple message. Not withstanding the poor season on the field, the club is currently in a stable position, and with a strategic plan that will enable us to adjust to future challenges. But what kind of club we have moving forward will depend on our ability to grow our crowds and our business, together with our ability to make more of what we already have and our capacity to be inventive and innovative. In simple terms we need more supporters, more Season Ticket holders, more commercial revenue, more Pridebuilder members, more Supporters' Trust members, yet more community engagement ,and yes we need to ensure that our marketing and communications plans are effective. We can only do these things with your help.

Finally, **Congratulations**   to our special guests from Folly Lane ARLFC, a club which I'm proud to say was founded by my dad and his pals back in 1946. This weekend they celebrate their 75th Anniversary, an occasion that Swinton Lions is very honoured to support.

SHEFFIELD EAGLES 28-34 SWINTON LIONS
13 September 2021

The Lions put in a stunning performance at the Keepmoat Stadium to claim their second victory of the season.

They got off to a great start after five minutes when some great passing across the line saw Luis Roberts dive over in the left corner for the opener, but Martyn Ridyard playing his three hundredth career game was unable to convert from the touchline. Five minutes later Nick Gregson latched onto a Sam Brooks pass to score under the posts and Ridyard made no mistake with the conversion.

Eagles hit back with a well worked try on fourteen minutes when Tyler Dickinson scored by the posts and Izaac Farrell added the conversion. Eagles' playmaker Anthony Thackeray had to leave the field with what looked like a dead leg just after this try and was never to return but it was the home side who went ahead on twenty-four minutes when Joel Farrell went over from close range and his brother added the conversion to put them ahead.

The next Eagles try came from Rob Worrincy when the Lions were forced into a goal line drop out, Ridyard's kick sailed straight into touch and from the play the ball ten metres out a long pass found the soon retiring winger to dive over in the corner but this time the conversion attempt from Farrell struck the posts and bounced out. This gave Sheffield a six-point advantage at the break.

The Lions started well again in the second half and Mitch Cox went very close to scoring having just returned from a HIA check, but it was Eagles who went further ahead when Swinton made a ball handing error near the Eagles line and winger Olly Butterworth swept up a stray pass to race eighty metres to score under the posts and Farrell converted this one.

From this point on the Lions took control of the game, with Reece Hamlett scoring his first Swinton try in the right corner and Ridyard added the conversion from the touchline.

Two more efforts from the Lions could have resulted in tries with firstly Mike Butt being held up on fifty-five minutes and then two minutes later Roberts crossed in the corner only to be brought back for a forward pass. However, the Lions did score on sixty-three minutes when a kick from Roberts bounced up nicely for the supporting Lewis Hatton and he fed the ball to Mitch Cox who raced in under the posts and Ridyard converted as the

scores were locked. Hamlett then almost created a second for the impressive Cox but again the pass was judged forward.

The Lions then took the lead on sixty-nine minutes when it was Cox the creator this time to send Geronimo Doyle over in the right corner and again Ridyard converted off the touchline. Three minutes later they were in again when some good build up play saw Hatton crash over under the posts and Ridyard converted this one too.

With two minutes left Ridyard attempted a drop goal, but the ball sailed wide and as the final hooter sounded the well beaten Eagles got over again with Joel Farrell scoring his second and Izaac adding the conversion. The Lions fans were ecstatic as the team went over to thank them after the game.

Ian Rigg at the Keepmoat Stadium

Lions:
Doyle, Hamlett, Lloyd, Butt, Roberts, Ridyard, Hansen, Brooks, Waterworth, Hatton, Gregson, Cox, Hope. (Subs) Brogan, Brickhill, Jones, Michael.

Stuart Fletcher added:
A big thank you to all our wonderful supporters who travelled to yesterday's game in numbers and never stopped getting behind the lads.

To see so many smiling faces at the end was fantastic and as Allan has already said that win for you all.

So proud of the coaching, backroom staff and the players who all work so hard during the week in training and deserve these moments

Please, if possible, get down to the Widnes game, bring family/friends and create our special atmosphere and cheer the boys to another victory
Thank you again

SWINTON LIONS 16-26 WIDNES VIKINGS
19 September 2021

The Vikings followed up their victory against the Bulls with a hard-fought win against the Lions which saw Matt Cook and Paul Clough make their final career  appearances and Referee Gareth Hewer controlling his last game before retirement.

The Vikings brought a large following and made a bright start stretching the Lions defence with their early attacks before Lions' hooker Luke Waterworth was held up on thirteen minutes. From the restart the ball moved swiftly left and Geronimo Doyle linked into the line to score on the wing, but Martyn Ridyard was unable to convert.

The Vikings hit back four minutes later when Lewis Else fed Adam Lawton to score on the left and Jack Owens converted. They scored again quickly when Deon Cross finished off a good passing movement to go over in the right corner, but Owens could not convert this one.

Will Hope had a good chance for the Lions four minutes from the break, but the ball went to ground with the line open and it was the Vikings who finished the half strongly when Lawton found Stephen Tyrer with a nice short pass and he went over in the corner, but again no conversion from Owens.

The Lions made an excellent start to the second half when some good build up passing led to Rhodri Lloyd finding the supporting Mitch Cox who raced away to score with Ridyard converting. They were starting to take control of the game, but it was the Vikings who scored next when they kept the ball alive on the last tackle and Jayden Hatton crossed on the left converted off the touchline by Owens.

Mike Butt looked all on to score on the left on the hour but a great tackle by Cross managed to knock him into touch. This seemed to change the momentum for the Vikings and Lewis Hulme went over from close range five minutes later again converted by Owens. Ben Heyes then pulled off a try saving tackle on Joe Lyons before Jake Spedding went over only to have the try cancelled out for a forward pass by Hatton.

The Lions scored the try of the match with just three minutes left after nearly all the team touched the ball before Reece Hamlett scored in the right corner and Ridyard added the conversion from the touchline, but it was too late to make any impression on the scoreboard. Both sides put on a guard of honour for Cook and Clough who have retired as they left the field.

Ian Rigg at Heywood Road

LIONS
22 Geronimo Doyle
21 Ben Heyes
11 Rhodri Lloyd
1 Mike Butt
39 Reece Hamlett
6 Martyn Ridyard
12 Nick Gregson
14 Billy Brickhill
9 Luke Waterworth
10 Lewis Hatton
3 Mitch Cox
13 Will Hope
15 Lewis Brogan
Subs (all used)

SWINTON LIONS V WIDNES VIKINGS
THE OFFICIAL MATCHDAY PROGRAMME

SWINTON LIONS R.L.F.C.
E.S.T 1866

BETFRED CHAMPIONSHIP

Fastflow
Energy Services Limited

BRAMPTON BREWERY

SUNDAY 19th SEPTEMBER 2021 | KICK OFF 15:00   ISSUE 14 | £3.00

24 Paul Nash
19 Deane Meadows
40 Ronan Michael
26 Jordan Brown
Tries: Doyle (23),
Cox (47), Hamlett
(77)
Goals: Ridyard 2/3

VIKINGS
Tries: Lawton (27),
Cross (31), Tyrer
(39), Hatton (53),
Hulme (65)
Goals: Owens 3/5

Right: Head coach
Allan Coleman
proudly presents
our steward Joseph
Eastham with a signed match ball. Joe enjoyed corporate with his mum
yesterday as part of a thank you for his prompt actions when David our club
president fell seriously ill at a recent game. Well done Joe!

Right: Jon Leeming of Brampton Brewery received a signed Swinton ball
from our head
coach Allan
Coleman. Thank
you once again to
Jon and his team
for sponsoring a
match ball here at
Swinton Lions!

Right: A huge thank you to Benn and Tony Cottrell and all at Fastflow Energy Services for their generous sponsorship of yesterday's match. Benn here is presented with a Lions shirt by our head coach Allan Coleman

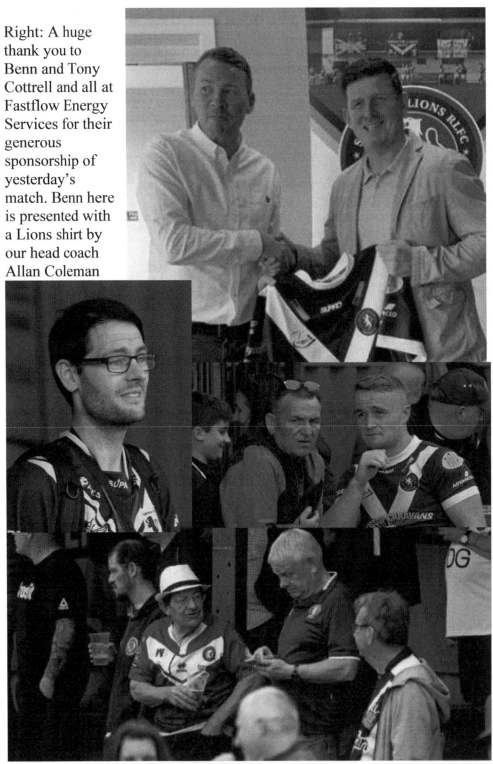

Above: Alan Marwick and Bob Hilton

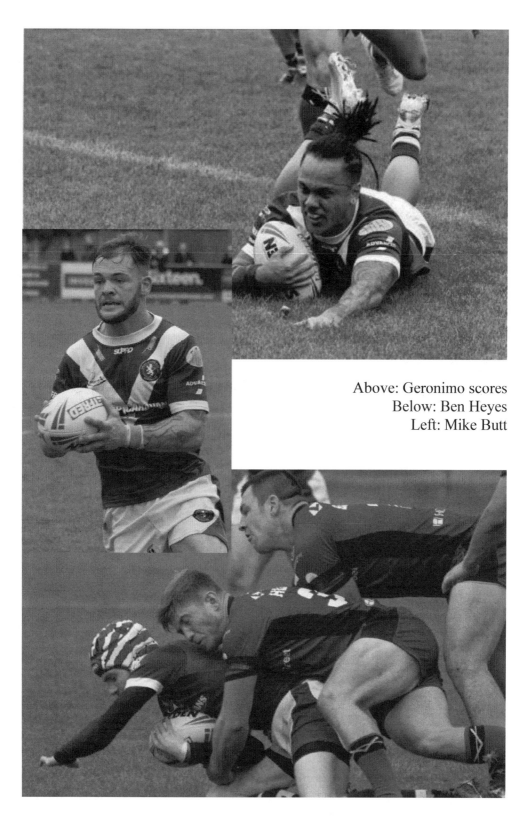

Above: Geronimo scores
Below: Ben Heyes
Left: Mike Butt

Above: Rhodri Lloyd gets past Matty Smith of the Vikings
Below: Martyn Ridyard

Above: Luke Waterworth
Right: Will Hope
Below: It's a wrap for the season!

REECE HAMLETT JOINS LIONS!
29 September 2021

Swinton Lions are delighted to reveal their first new signing of 2022 – Reece Hamlett!

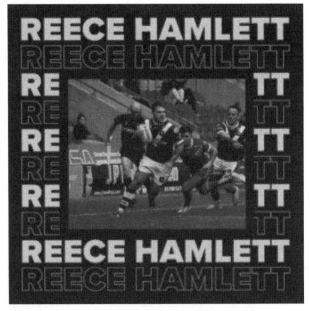

Lions' CEO **Steve Wild** said, "We are thrilled to formally welcome Reece to the club, who of course is well known to our fans having already appeared at both centre and wing this year whilst on loan from Bradford Bulls. At the back end of the season Reece added a bit of extra steel and pace to our three-quarter line in both attack and defence, and our coach Allan Coleman was keen to get him to the club on a permanent basis.

"It's therefore fantastic news to have Reece on board, and in that respect I must pay tribute to our Pridebuilder scheme, whose members have once again been central to this recruitment."

Swinton Lions Head Coach **Allan Coleman** added, "I've known Reece for a good number of years now, in fact from about the age of 13. Reece is a powerful player and he fits into how I want our team to play next year. I think he's already demonstrated to our fans that he wants to be part of the Swinton Lions family, and I can't wait to work with him in pre-season and get the best out of Reece Hamlett in 2022."

Reece himself was also delighted at signing for the Lions. He said, "I can't wait to start the new season at Swinton Lions. During my time on loan at the club I really felt at home and welcomed by a fantastic team of players and staff.

"The playing style at Swinton really suits me and I think I'll find some great form there, and help the Lions get back up into the Championship where they belong. I'd like to thank everyone at Swinton for their help in getting the deal done, and I'm really excited to see what the next 12 months holds."

Welcome Reece to Swinton Lions!

End of Season Awards

The end of season awards evening was held after the final game of the season against Widnes. Amongst the Lions and Lionesses being presented with awards were:

Player of the Year	Mike Butt
Player Of the Year 2nd Place: Rhodri Lloyd	3rd Place Nick Gregson
Man of Steel	Mitch Cox
Young Player of the Year	Louis Brogan
Player's Player of the Year	Geronimo Doyle
Coaches Player of the Year	Mike Butt
Club Person of the Year	Lyndsey Watkins
Champagne Moment and Try of the Season	Jack Hansen's try v Dewsbury
Leading Try Scorer	Mike Butt

A few photos from the enjoyable social evening:

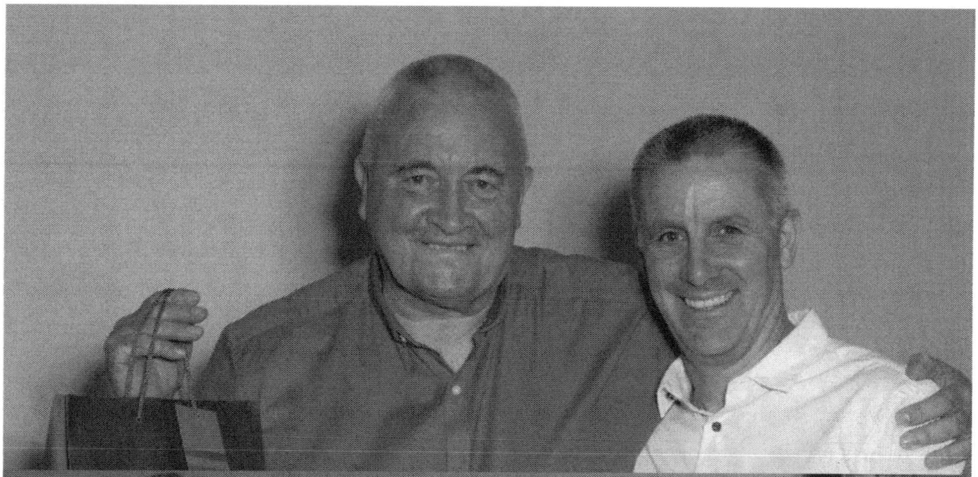

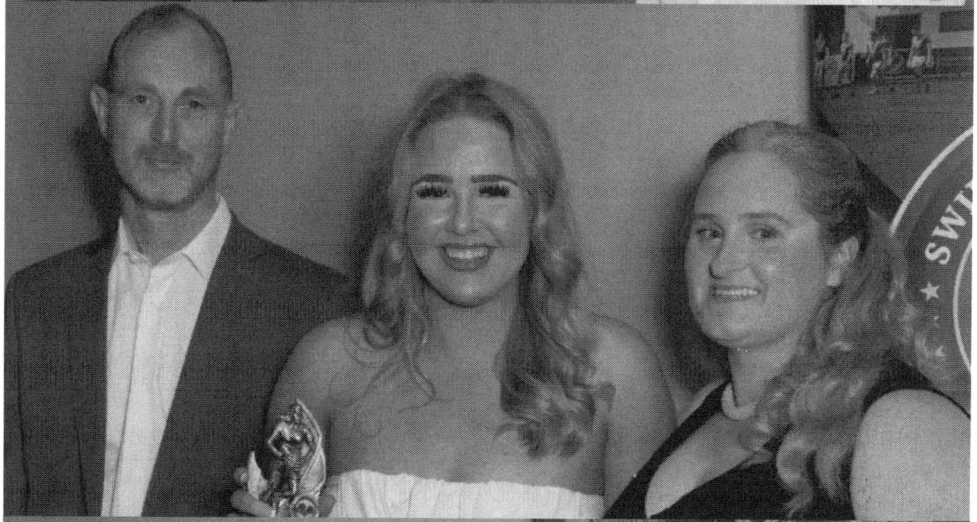

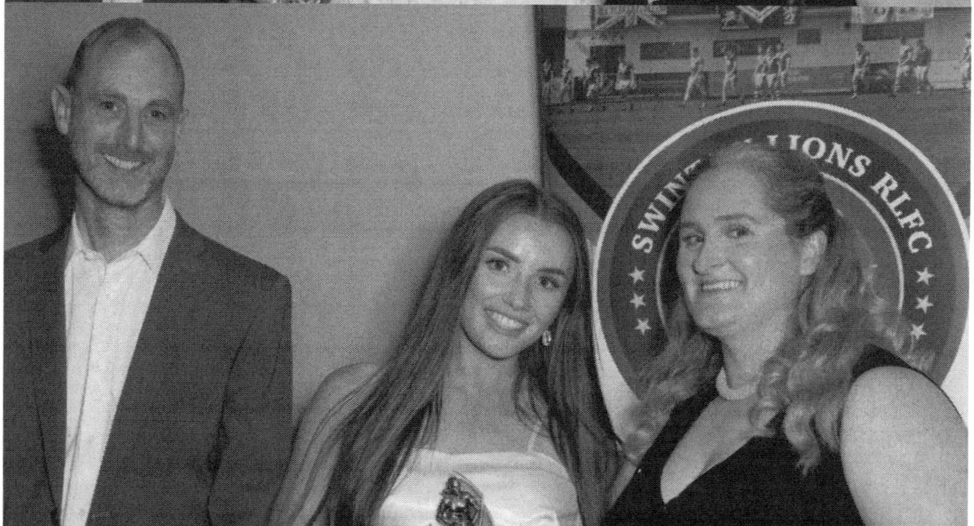

Diary of a Season 2021 – Swinton Lions

End of Season Thoughts

Ian Bailey

I've been a supporter of the Lions for over fifty years but things could have been a lot different for me because I was born into a family of Salford Rugby fans but my mother and father moved to the Borough of Swinton & Pendlebury where I was born. So as a very young boy my father would take me to the Willows, which meant I missed out on the great Swinton team of the sixties but when I was old enough, I started to go to Station Road where my love affair with the Lions began.

Over the years I've seen a lot of ups and downs, winning the Second Division Premiership at Old Trafford, the Second Division Championship, promotions and relegations , the loss of Station Road , 30 years nomadic existence , the fantastic experiences of watching the Lions in Canada and France and now at Sale which again as seen us have ups and downs. But before the start of this season for the first time in a long time I was looking forward to a good season from us, with what looked like one of our strongest squads in years but being Swinton things have not quite turned out that way, Covid has not helped and we've had probably the worst injury list I can ever recall in my time following the Lions, which has resulted in some very disappointing results and performance's and it looks like we are now facing relegation which In turn will result in another fight for survival for the club .

Which at the start of this season nobody saw that coming, fingers crossed we can regroup and rebuild to face whatever battles there are to overcome 📷

Stuart Latham

Well, this was not quite what was hoped for this season, but you need to focus on the positives. Looking back on recent seasons at least the club is still going and has a secure grounding for moving forward in the future. We have a good working relationship with Sale Rugby Club which ensures we can work together happily in the next seasons as we plan our recovery.

As to results on the pitch, everyone has their own opinion, and I think its best left to Steve Wild and Stuart Fletcher to pass comment on this. But I will say that we have the best fans in the league, who stood together with the club through thick and thin and are loyal to the core and came back week after week to support the club. People like Mark Cull who made the journey every week from his home in Crewe to wear our colours and shout for the lions.

Even at the Widnes game with bottom place in the league a certainty there was a "Gallows" style humour in the stands by the fans who had attended, and it was comical to listen to the views knowing those commenting would be back supporting the team next season. Yes, the fans definitely retained their sense of humour throughout. If anyone doubted it, you only had to come up to the corporate area and join in a conversation with the likes of Ian Bailey; Howard Sloane and Glenn Roberts to see that the club has a great future assisted by loyal stewards including Paul Leadbeater and Daniel Thomson and the efforts of Rhys Griffiths, Stephen Parker and Tracey Parker working with the Pride Builder and Supporter's Club must also be mentioned. The photography skills of Peter Green and Emily Parker also needs to be recorded and their efforts are on show in this book. If I were to mention everyone involved the book would dramatically increase in size but it has been a fantastic effort from all associated with the club off the pitch as without their efforts, there would be no club!

Moving forward, the club's base has been established in Sale and a good fan base is growing as we establish roots in the town, so in uncertain times for the sport, everyone at Swinton can look forward to the future.

This book has received a positive response from the fans, had the season been more successful then, sales would no doubt have been higher, but with profits aiding the clubs attempts to have a memorable season on the pitch in 2022 I leave the thought with you that this "yearbook" could become an annual event if required and I look to writing a sequel next year to again aide the club financially.

Mark Richardson

I'm sure it's the same for many fans. I sit down in the stand and a shiver goes down my spine. The memories of Station Rd and attending games with granddad and father in law, none of whom are with us anymore, and the lump in my throat comes and then eventually goes.

I don't ever want that feeling to leave me.

I love my club. I love the fans I chat to, Jane Huxley, Tim Hughes, Tim Fensome, Amy Fensome, Raymond Cresswell, Ian Rigg some in passing ,some for ages. I love taking the piss out of Pete Green and his weird culinary habits. I love Mike Butt giving absolutely 100% to entertain me.

I admire the commitment of Stuart Fletcher, Stephen Wild, Stephen Parker and Tracey Parker-Drinkwater .

It's been an absolutely crap season but the last few performances under Allan Coleman fill me with hope. Who knows what the RFL will throw at us but I'll be there next year.

It's in my blood.

I get emotional at every game as I remember and miss the great men in my in my life and the joy and more often the heartache we shared.

Roll on 2022. It can only get better.

Steve Wild

CEO Steve Wild looks back on the 2021 Season

Season 2021 will be long remembered at Swinton Lions for a variety of reasons, sadly much of which will be against a backdrop of relegation at a time when otherwise there is so much to be proud of at the club.

Preparations for season 2021 began last November against the spectre of the covid pandemic. Covid-19 protocols and procedures were plentiful and highly complex, and involved various risk assessments, daily health questionnaires, revised operational directives and a whole variety of essential paperwork. And that was just to get back on the training ground at the AJ Bell Stadium! Sadly the resumption of training didn't last long and we were soon back under lockdown, but from January we were slowly able to resume our pre-season preparations, albeit still under strict covid guidelines.

A return to the playing of competitive matches added yet another layer of complexity, but after a number of sleepless nights dealing with yet more complex protocol, and in consultation with our stadium hosts Sale FC, we were given the all clear to play games behind closed doors – something which would not have been possible but for a fantastic and willing band of volunteers.

On the field the 2021 campaign started with some promise. An away success at Bradford Bulls in a pre-season friendly was followed by victories over Newcastle and Oldham in the 1895 Cup (doubling as the first two rounds of the Challenge Cup), and suddenly we were just 80 minutes from a first ever trip to Wembley!

The league season began at Oldham, and with it came defeat due to a second half when everything that could go wrong went wrong. That loss however then seemed to set the tone for what was to come, a situation exacerbated by a number of serious injuries to key personnel that quickly mounted up. Our marquee signing Liam Forsyth was sidelined for months, as were other key players Lewis Hatton, Richard Lepori and Jose Kenga. Many others were in and out of the team due to injuries, covid and suspension.

In the meantime off the field some fantastic progress was being made. The formation of our two female Lionesses teams was a landmark moment for the club, as was the setting up of our junior section, the Manchester Lions, as part of the driving force behind the Greater Manchester Player Development League. The club was then confirmed as an official England Talent Pathway Partner, another huge development. The club was certainly getting noticed across the Rugby League world, and being seen as proactive and innovative.

Our training facilities were also given a boost when we secured a lease for gym and office accommodation at the AJ Bell Stadium, alongside outside pitch space. Ironically the situation had been forced by covid and our need to have our own protected bio environment, but nevertheless we are now in possession of some of the best training facilities outside of Super League.

In mid-May at last we could welcome crowds back to Heywood Road, although to begin with we were restricted to a ground capacity of just 580. Unfortunately the big welcome back to crowds evening became a frustrating experience, as Dewsbury emerged with a narrow two-points success.

The Wembley dream ended at York in the semi-finals of the 1895 Cup, and a few weeks later the Board took the tough decision to part company with head coach Sturt Littler, who had served the club with dignity and distinction in different capacities for the previous 6 years. He was replaced by assistant coach Allan Coleman, who immediately gained a first league success of the season, thanks to an incredible last minute winner by Jack Hansen at Dewsbury.

Matters were put into perspective in June when our club President, David Jones, suffered a cardiac arrest during the match against Newcastle Thunder at Heywood Road. Thankfully the swift action of our staff saved David's life, and at the time of preparing these notes David continues to make a good recovery.

As the injured players returned, the squad strengthened, and results improved. Sadly it was too late to get out of the bottom two and we now look set to begin 2022 in the third tier of the game.

However, we will continue to build our club and our culture at Swinton Lions. The pandemic has been managed sensibly from a financial perspective, and despite the huge challenges facing the game, particularly from the expected huge drop in central distribution, we are not in a bad place to face the future. We also have an incredibly loyal bunch of fans, as demonstrated by our superb Supporters'' Trust and Pridebuilder organisations.

The Board therefore is confident that not only will Swinton Lions survive the immediate future, but it will continue to evolve and stay relevant, and consequently play an important part in the sport of Rugby League moving forwards.

Stuart Fletcher

As the 2021 season concludes there is no down time or respite as its business as usual behind the scenes.

There are frequent meetings held by the RFL with Championship and League one Clubs in relation to the future structure of the sport in conjunction with the new SKY broadcasting partnership and the impact that will have on each club

on its central funding allocation. These meetings are lively with constructive debate and each Club has opportunity to put proposals forward to assist in shaping the sport. These meetings are ongoing and forms part of the regular dialogue the Club has with the Governing Body on numerous subjects.

What is clear is that the central funding the Club will receive in 2022 will be considerably less than in 2021 and detailed financial planning takes place to put together a competitive budget. Meetings takes place with Allan, Head Coach, to agree a playing staff budget that is competitive but takes into account the Central Funding reductions and doesn't put the future of club at stake. This financial management is ongoing throughout the year and very detailed.

Discussions take place with players the Club has targeted, and these discussions take time as with some players agents are involved and negotiations take place in putting the 2022 squad together in line with the playing budget.

Being a professional Club is not about just receiving Central Funding it is about being 'relevant 'to the sport and generating other revenue streams. This is ongoing and involves generating various sponsorship with business partners together with regular discussions with Pride builder and the Supporters Trust and communication with general base through forum[s]. Podcasts and social media.

Another part of being 'relevant 'is the community work delivered by the Club. Increasing participation and involvement with the sport. The work undertaken by the Foundation has grown throughout 2021 and will continue going forward. The Manchester Lions and Lionesses have been a huge success and will develop further. The Clubs Community Partnership with our five community clubs has assisted those Clubs grow and will continue.

The Governance of the Club is pivotal in driving forward our Business strategy and plans and through Board meetings and working closely with Head Coach our aims and objectives reviewed constantly to ensure has vision and targets met.

 internal work is ongoing to improve our various social media platforms, communication with all our stakeholders, commercial brochure, sponsorship networking events. Planning constantly takes place towards 2022 and beyond an example being of improving match day experiences for the demographic of our fan base including season tickets/match day initiatives

This I hope gives a flavour of the work that continues from season 2021 into the following year and it really is 24/7 in leading our fantastic, historic club, a club I first attended in 1969 standing on the terraces at Station Road and like so many the Club runs in my veins.

Season 2021 may not have gone how everyone wanted but what is impressive is the way everyone has stuck together and shows why our fans are the best in the sport in my view and why our family ethos will drive us forward and show the rugby league community what Swinton Lions are all about.

I personally thank all our playing, coaching and backroom staff, our business partners , sponsors , fellow Directors , Pride builder and Supporters Trust members and last but not least our general fan base for the commitment in 2021 and look  forward in leading the club in 2022.

Stuart Fletcher
Chairman

Rhodri Lloyd

2021 didn't go to plan for our beloved Swinton Lions, and like the fans us players were not happy at all with the outcome of our season.

Our season began with high hopes we had impressive wins in preseason friendlies agonist a strong Bradford side who finished the season in the top 4 and wins against Newcastle and Oldham in the cup. However, our season was halted there with a 11-game losing run. A losing run is very difficult to overcome, it can be hard to mentally stay upbeat especially after the narrow defeats we suffered against Dewsbury and Bradford, as a captain it was a challenge to keep the players motivated and upbeat. Especially with having a large number of the salary cap injured with long term injuries, it felt as if everything was against us.

The board came to the decision that a change was needed, although I and the players take full responsibility to our performances on the pitch, Stuart was dealt the short straw and was let go. Decisions like that can go either way, luckily for us it worked, and we managed to get a couple of wins for you fans at the back end of the season.

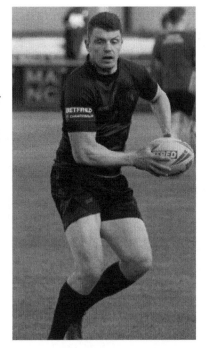

Alan Coleman is a great coach and has come with new ideas and it's looking promising for next season, I am aiming high for us lions next year, there's pressure on us and we must thrive under that pressure.

The biggest thing of all for 2022 is to get back to winning ways and see the Lions faithful smiling, and victoriously.

The Supporter's Club
Pride Builder

Swinton Lions Pride Builder Fund - The 2021 season

The Swinton Lions Pride Builder fund is a fan's led initiative that raises money for the sole purpose of helping the Club to strengthen its' playing squad. It was launched in April 2018 in response to the club's financial situation at that time. The fund is run by fans, it is independent of the Club and the money raised is therefore protected from creditors.

Swinton Lions Pride Builder
Sort Code: 30-92-92
Account No: 37544168

The number of available quality players is relatively small and competition between clubs for the best of them is keen. As professional sportsmen, players and their agents know their monetary worth and when deciding which club to sign for, ultimately the amount of money on offer is a key factor. This is why the Pride Builder fund is key to the fortunes of the club.

To become a member of Pride Builder all you need to do is set up a regular bank transfer or standing order to the fund. The details are shown on the logo. Members receive **exclusive** regular updates of the fund's incomings and outgoings, fund raising initiatives, new signings and other club news.

Since being established in 2018 the Pride Builder fund has helped the club to secure the signings of Will Hope, Gavin Bennion, Paddy Jones and Oscar Thomas. It has also contributed to (or fully funded) the loan or dual registration signings of Ilias Bergal, Craig Mullen, Josh Woods, Liam Paisley, Rob Fairclough, Nick Gregson and many others.

2021: Due to the ongoing generosity of the fans during the curtailed 2020 season, the Pride Builder built up a healthy bank balance which was made available to the club for its 2021 recruitment plans. The fund helped towards paying the 3rd year option of Will Hope's contract plus the pre-season signings of Liam Forsyth, Martin Ridyard, Sam Brooks and Geronimo Doyle. Pride Builder also financed the loan signing of Sam Luckley.

Sadly, Liam Forsyth missed almost the whole of the league season due to injury and the other 4 players have all missed games through injury, illness, Covid protocols and suspension. Everybody associated with the Club shares the disappointment with this season's results on the pitch and the lack of on-field success has doubtless been a factor in over a dozen former regular donors suspending their contributions. However, a couple have recently resumed their payments and incredibly more fans have set up new regular bank transfers. The membership currently stands at 109 individuals.

2022 and beyond: With relegation all but a certainty and central funding due to be reduced, the importance of alternative income streams to help the club survive and hopefully prosper has never been greater. The Pride Builder fund has quickly become a fundamental part of the Club's budget planning and with the fans' loyal and generous support this will hopefully continue well into the future.

If you are not already a member and you want to help the Club attract quality players, simply set up a regular bank transfer to the Pride Builder fund. We also always welcome any fundraising initiatives. Name cards, corporate meal raffle prizes, race nights, duck races, merchandise sales etc. have all helped to swell the Pride Builder coffers.

For further details or information just speak to any of the Pride Builder admin team (Tim Fensome, Dave Roberts or Rhys Griffiths) or email pridebuilder@outlook.com

Above: Rhys Griffiths

The Swinton Lions Supporters Trust

The Supporters' Trust was established in 2002 at a critical time in the history of the Lions when Swinton supporters with help from the wider rugby league family rallied together to help those left to run the club to ensure there was a Club for the future. The club then subsequently offered the Trust a place on the Club board in return for their financial support and shares in the club, a position that was taken by Steve Wild who has been involved ever since and is now the current Club CEO and Operations Director. In 2019 following the most recent boardroom shuffle the re-structured board now includes our current Trust Chair Stephen Parker who also assists in some of the day-to-day Club work.

Membership of the Trust is open to anyone for the low amount of a min. £2/month or £24/year as the Trust must be affordable to all. We, as a Society Registered under the Co-Operative & Community Benefit Societies Act, we hold regular meetings, record all our financial affairs and are regulated by the FCA. The current board of the Trust consists of several long-standing Swinton supporters whose skill set enable the Trust to operate as an effective partner to the Club.

But enough of the official stuff as we are much more than that. Not only does the Trust provide financial support to the Club we also provide support to the wider rugby league community and have throughout the years sponsored kits for our local community Club Folly Lane ARLFC, recently assisted in paying for pitch-side fencing and donated gifts to other local fundraising community organisations.

Monies are raised not only through our regular subscriptions but also through regular fundraising activities such as quiz and bingo events, social events & dinners, merchandise sales, heritage events, stalls at local community events and festivals. Having a presence at these events allows us to promote not only the work of the Trust but share the love we have for the Swinton Lions.

Trust members also take an active role during match-days from having people at the gates, producing and selling programmes, raffle ticket selling, club and trust pop-up merchandise shop running, setting out corporate décor, club signage and advertising and stewarding.

We also help our mascot Dana the Lion carry out his regular duties of not only attending on match-days but special visits on community days, events and special occasions, like the annual Christmas Party for our Junior Lion fans.

What we do need more of are Trust members and in turn from these, more people on the board especially those who can add value to our work and want to be more hands-on for us. There is always a need to re-fresh the Trust and a shout goes out for more to join us to enable us to do more. New members and additional ideas for things we can do are always welcome as we strive to make our club and our rugby league community the best possible.
Join the Trust. Get your family and friends to join the Trust. Help us do more for the Club and community. #lionsfamily Follow all social media channels for information and up-coming events…..

www.lionstrust.co.uk
@lionstrust on twitter and
Instagram

LIONSTRUST

The Fans

A big thank you to the fans who have supported the club through thick and thin. See you all next season!

End of Season Stats

2020 Season

Results and league table from the season that ended suddenly through Covid.

Match Date	Opposition	Competition	Home/ Away	Score
5 January	Salford Red Devils	Friendly	Away	52-4
25 January	Warrington Wolves	Friendly	Home	16-12
2 February	Whitehaven	Betfred Championship	Away	14-0
16 February	Batley Bulldogs	Betfred Championship	Away	20-10
22 February	Leigh Miners Rangers	Coral Challenge Cup	Home	56-0
8 March	Featherstone Rovers	Betfred Championship	Away	35-24
15 March	Widnes Vikings	Coral Challenge Cup	Away	32-16

#	Name	Played	Won	Drawn	Lost	For	Against	Points
1	Toulouse Olympique	5	5	0	0	180	48	10
2	Leigh Centurions	4	4	0	0	162	40	8
3	Featherstone Rovers	4	4	0	0	137	74	8
4	London Broncos	5	4	0	1	92	28	8
5	Widnes Vikings	5	3	0	2	92	36	6
6	Dewsbury Rams	4	3	0	1	72	66	6
7	Bradford Bulls	4	2	0	2	90	60	4
8	Halifax	4	2	0	2	82	73	4
9	Batley Bulldogs	5	1	0	4	82	133	3
10	Swinton Lions	3	1	0	2	48	55	2
11	Sheffield Eagles	5	1	0	4	60	148	2
12	Oldham	5	1	0	4	46	158	2
13	York City Knights	4	0	0	4	26	102	0
14	Whitehaven	5	0	0	5	54	146	0

2021 Season
Betfred Championship Table

	Name	Pld	W	L	D	P F	P A	PTS
1	Toulouse Olympique XIII	14	14	0	0	698	124	28
2	Featherstone Rovers	21	20	1	0	943	292	38
3	Halifax Panthers	21	13	8	0	528	354	26
4	Batley Bulldogs	21	13	8	0	561	411	26
5	Bradford Bulls	20	12	8	0	514	501	24
6	Whitehaven RLFC	22	12	9	1	502	524	25
7	London Broncos	20	11	8	1	552	579	21
8	Widnes Vikings	21	9	11	1	494	534	19
9	York City Knights	20	9	11	0	502	477	18
10	Dewsbury Rams	21	8	12	1	360	608	17
11	Newcastle Thunder	20	7	12	1	431	627	15
12	Sheffield Eagles	20	5	12	3	420	665	13
13	Oldham RLFC	21	2	18	1	308	748	5
14	Swinton Lions	22	2	19	1	404	773	5

Betfred Championship Results
SUN 19TH SEPTEMBER 2021

Swinton Lions 16 26 Widnes Vikings

Round: 22 Venue: Heywood Road

SUN 12TH SEPTEMBER 2021

Sheffield Eagles 28 34 Swinton Lions

Round: 21 Venue: Keepmoat Stadium

SUN 5TH SEPTEMBER 2021

Swinton Lions 32 34 London Broncos

Round: 20 Venue: Heywood Road

SUN 29TH AUGUST 2021

Halifax Panthers 48 12 Swinton Lions

Round: 19 Venue: The Shay Stadium

SUN 22ND AUGUST 2021

Bradford Bulls 30 26 Swinton Lions

Round: 18 Venue: Odsal Stadium

SUN 15TH AUGUST 2021

Swinton Lions 6 38 Batley Bulldogs

Round: 17 Venue: Heywood Road

SUN 8TH AUGUST 2021

Swinton Lions 22 22 Oldham RLFC

Round: 16 Venue: Heywood Road

SUN 1ST AUGUST 2021

Dewsbury Rams 18 22 Swinton Lions

Round: 15 Venue: Tetley's Stadium

SUN 25TH JULY 2021

York City Knights **46** **10** Swinton Lions

Round: 14 Venue: LNER Community Stadium

SUN 11TH JULY 2021

Swinton Lions **22** **30** Sheffield Eagles

Round: 13 Venue: Heywood Road

SUN 4TH JULY 2021

Whitehaven RLFC **36** **22** Swinton Lions

Round: 12 Venue: Recreation Ground

SUN 27TH JUNE 2021

London Broncos **38** **24** Swinton Lions

Round: 11 Venue: Trailfinders Sports Club

SUN 20TH JUNE 2021

Swinton Lions **4** **34** Halifax Panthers

Round: 10 Venue: Heywood Road

SUN 13TH JUNE 2021

Swinton Lions   30 36   Newcastle Thunder

Round: 9 Venue: Heywood Road

SUN 30TH MAY 2021

Batley Bulldogs   26 12   Swinton Lions

Round: 8 Venue: The Fox's Biscuit Stadium

SAT 22ND MAY 2021

Toulouse Olympique XIII   66 18   Swinton Lions

Round: 7 Venue: Heywood Road

MON 17TH MAY 2021

Swinton Lions   18 20   Dewsbury Rams

Round: 6 Venue: Heywood Road

SUN 9TH MAY 2021

Swinton Lions   22 23   Bradford Bulls

Round: 5 Venue: Heywood Road

SUN 2ND MAY 2021

Widnes Vikings **46** | **10** Swinton Lions

Round: 4 Venue: Halton Stadium

SUN 25TH APRIL 2021

Swinton Lions **16** | **64** York City Knights

Round: 3 Venue: Heywood Road

SUN 18TH APRIL 2021

Swinton Lions **6** | **36** Featherstone Rovers

Round: 2 Venue: Heywood Road

FRI 2ND APRIL 2021

Oldham RLFC **28** | **20** Swinton Lions

Round: 1 Venue: Bower Fold

BetFred Challenge Cup

SUN 11TH APRIL 2021

Swinton Lions **8** | **32** Warrington Wolves

Round: 3 Venue: Heywood Road

SUN 28TH MARCH 2021

Swinton Lions 23 14 Oldham RLFC

Round: 2 Venue: Heywood Road

SUN 21ST MARCH 2021

Swinton Lions 28 16 Newcastle Thunder

Round: 1 Venue: Heywood Road

AB Sundecks 1895 Cup

SUN 6TH JUNE 2021

York City Knights 36 22 Swinton Lions

AB Sundecks 1895 Cup Round: Semi Finals

Venue: LNER Community Stadium

Season's Stats

Name	Played	Sub	Tries	Goals	Drop Goals	Points
Billy Brickhill	10	9	2			8
Louis Brogan	15	7	2			8
Sam Brooks	15	3	1			4
Jordan Brown	1	7				
Tayler Brown		9				
Owen Buckley	4		2			8
Mike Butt	23		11			44
Dan Clare	1					
Mitch Cox	26		9			36
Geronimo Doyle	21		4			16
Liam Forsyth	1					
Sam Grant	2	1	1			4
Cobi Green	7	6	1			4
Nick Gregson	21	1	3	2		16
Reece Hamlett	5		2			8
Jack Hansen	24		8	7		46
Lewis Hatton	10		4			16
Ben Heyes	6	3	4			16
Will Hope	20	2	4			16
Dominic Horn		1				
Paddy Jones	2	17				
Jose Kenga						
Richard Lepori	4					
Rhodri Lloyd	25		7			28
Sam Luckley	3	1				
Deane Meadows	9	10	4			16
Ronan Michael	4	7	1			4
Paul Nash	1	13	1			4
Martyn Ridyard	23		3	59	1	131
Nico Rizzelli	3		2			8
Luis Roberts	20		10			40
Tom Spencer	6	6				
Luke Waterworth	25		1			4
Total	26		87	68	1	485

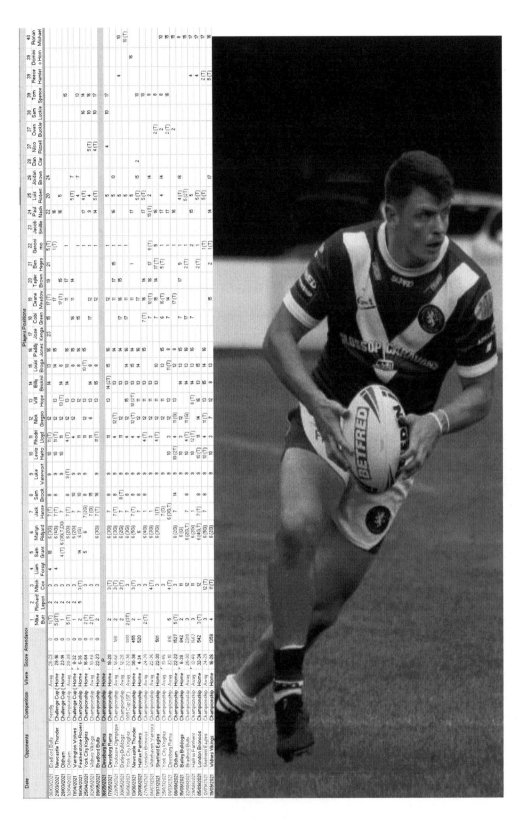

Date	Opponents	Competition	Where	Score	Attendance
06/03/2021	Bradford Bulls	Friendly	Away	28-22	0
21/03/2021	Newcastle Thunder	Challenge Cup	Home	36-16	0
28/03/2021	Oldham	Challenge Cup	Home	23-14	0
02/04/2021	Oldham	Championship	Away	26-28	0
11/04/2021	Warrington Wolves	Challenge Cup	Home	6-32	0
18/04/2021	Featherstone Rovers	Championship	Home	6-36	0
25/04/2021	York City Knights	Championship	Home	16-64	0
02/05/2021	Widnes Vikings	Championship	Away	10-48	0
09/05/2021	Bradford Bulls	Championship	Home	22-23	0
16/05/2021	Dewsbury Rams	Championship	Home	18-20	
17/05/2021	Dewsbury Rams	Championship	Home	18-20	
22/05/2021	Toulouse Olympique	Championship	Away	18-62	986
30/05/2021	Batley Bulldogs	Championship	Home	12-28	
06/06/2021	York City Knights	1895 Cup (SF)	Away	22-36	1451
13/06/2021	Newcastle Thunder	Championship	Home	30-36	495
20/06/2021	Halifax Panthers	Championship	Home	4-34	520
27/06/2021	London Broncos	Championship	Away	24-36	
04/07/2021	Whitehaven	Championship	Away	22-36	
19/07/2021	Sheffield Eagles	Championship	Home	22-30	501
25/07/2021	York City Knights	Championship	Away	19-46	
01/08/2021	Dewsbury Rams	Championship	Away	22-16	616
08/08/2021	Oldham	Championship	Away	22-22	
15/08/2021	Batley Bulldogs	Championship	Home	6-38	1527
22/08/2021	Bradford Bulls	Championship	Away	26-30	842
29/08/2021	Halifax Panthers	Championship	Home	6-29	2319
05/09/2021	London Broncos	Championship	Home	32-34	1663
12/09/2021	Sheffield Eagles	Championship	Away	24-23	542
19/09/2021	Widnes Vikings	Championship	Home	16-26	1358

Diary of a Season 2021 – Swinton Lions

Honours

Rugby League Championship	WINNERS, 1927, 1928, 1931, 1935, 1963, 1964. RUNNERS-UP, 1925, 1933, 1940.
Challenge Cup	WINNERS, 1900, 1926, 1928. RUNNERS-UP, 1927, 1932.
Lancashire Cup	WINNERS, 1925-26, 1927-28, 1939-40, 1969-70. RUNNERS-UP, 1910-11, 1923-24, 1931-32, 1960-61, 1961-62, 1962-63, 1964-65, 1972-73.
Lancashire League	WINNERS, 1925, 1928, 1929, 1931, 1940, 1961. RUNNERS-UP, 1893(RFU), 1894(RFU), 1898, 1901, 1923, 1927, 1935, 1939, 1966.
Western Division Championship	RUNNERS-UP, 1964.
BBC2 Floodlit Trophy	RUNNERS-UP, 1966-67.
2nd Division Championship (2nd Tier)	WINNERS, 1985. RUNNERS-UP, 1987. PROMOTED, 1975, 1991.
2nd Division Premiership (2nd Tier)	WINNERS, 1987. RUNNERS-UP, 1989.
League One (3rd Tier)	WINNERS, 2011. RUNNERS-UP, 1996, 2006(Play-off Finalists), 2015 (Play-Off Winners).
iPro Sport League 1 Cup	RUNNERS-UP, 2015
Wigan Sevens	WINNERS, 1985

Records

Appearances and Career Points	Ken Gowers (602 Apps & 2105 Points)
Season and Match Points	Ian Mort (338 Season & 48 Match)
Career and Season Tries	Jim Valentine (301 Career 48.Season)
Match Tries	Mark Riley (6)
Career Goals	Ken Gowers (970)
Season Goals	Albert Blan (128)
Match Goals	Ian Mort (14)
Record Attendance	26,891 (1964)